ANDROID APP DEVELOPMENT

FOR

ADVANCED DEVELOPERS

Master Jetpack, MVVM, AI, Performance Optimization, and Build Real-World Apps

Wilson Hayes

Copyright © 2025 by Wilson Hayes

TABLE OF CONTENTS

Introduction

Welcome to Advanced Android Development

Android is the **most widely used** mobile operating system, powering billions of devices globally. From simple apps to complex enterprise solutions, the demand for **skilled Android developers** continues to grow.

If you've built beginner-level Android apps and want to **take your skills to the next level**, this book is for you.

This **Advanced Edition** will help you build **high-performance, scalable, and feature-rich Android applications**. By the time you finish, you'll be comfortable with **modern development practices**, from Jetpack Compose to AI-powered apps.

However, before diving into advanced topics, let's **recap the fundamental concepts** from beginner-level Android development.

Recap of Beginner-Level Concepts

This book assumes you have **basic Android development knowledge**. If you're unfamiliar with these concepts, I highly recommend referring to my **beginner's book**:

Android App Development for Beginners: Master Java, Kotlin, and Android Studio to Build Fully Functional, Real-World Mobile Apps from Scratch

1. Java & Kotlin Basics

- **Java:** Object-oriented, powerful, but verbose.

- **Kotlin:** Google's recommended language, with less boilerplate and safer null handling.

Need a refresher on Kotlin? Check out Chapter X in *Android App Development for Beginners*.

2. Android Studio & Project Structure

- Android Studio is the **official IDE** for Android development.

- Key components:

  o **Manifest file** – Declares app components and permissions.

- o **res/layout** – Defines UI using XML or Jetpack Compose.

- o **Gradle files** – Manages dependencies and builds.

3. Activity & Fragment Lifecycle

- Android apps are **event-driven**, meaning the system controls when they start, pause, resume, or stop.

- **Activity Lifecycle:**

java

```
@Override

protected void onCreate(Bundle savedInstanceState) {

    super.onCreate(savedInstanceState);

    setContentView(R.layout.activity_main);

}
```

- **Fragments:** Reusable UI components inside Activities.

Not sure how Activities and Fragments work? Revisit Chapter X of *Android App Development for Beginners*.

4. UI Design with XML & Jetpack Compose

- **XML layouts:** The traditional method for UI design.

- **Jetpack Compose:** A modern declarative UI framework using Kotlin.

Need help with XML layouts before switching to Jetpack Compose? Chapter X in *Android App Development for Beginners* covers this in detail.

5. Data Storage & API Integration

- **SQLite & Room Database** for local data.

- **SharedPreferences** for small key-value storage.

- **Retrofit** for making API calls.

Case Study: A weather app fetches live data from an API using Retrofit.

If all these concepts feel **familiar**, you're ready to dive into **advanced Android development**.

Overview of Advanced Android Development

Why Go Beyond the Basics?

Many developers stop after learning how to build **basic CRUD (Create, Read, Update, Delete) apps**. But in real-world development, you need **more than just beginner skills** to succeed.

Advanced Android development is about:

- **Creating high-performance, scalable apps**

- **Building modular, maintainable architectures**

- **Enhancing UI/UX with Jetpack Compose & animations**

- **Implementing real-time features (WebSockets, Firebase, AI/ML)**

- **Optimizing apps for speed, battery efficiency, and security**

What You'll Learn in This Book

This book covers **everything you need to master advanced Android development**, including:

- **Modern UI Design:** Jetpack Compose, animations, custom views.

- **MVVM & Clean Architecture:** Writing scalable, modular code.

- **Networking & APIs:** WebSockets, GraphQL, Firebase Firestore.

- **Security & Testing:** Biometric authentication, ProGuard, CI/CD pipelines.

- **Monetization & Publishing:** In-app purchases, ads, app store optimization.

- **AI & Machine Learning:** Chatbots, AI recommendations, TensorFlow Lite.

By the end, you won't just **know how to code**—you'll be ready to **build professional-grade apps** used by millions.

Who Is This Book For? (Target Audience)

This book is for **developers who already understand basic Android development** and want to:

- **Take their skills to a professional level**

- **Build real-world applications with advanced features**

- **Learn best practices and optimize performance**

Ideal Readers:

- **Junior Android Developers** – Wanting to transition to intermediate/advanced level.

- **Freelancers & Indie Developers** – Looking to build and monetize Android apps.

- **Startup Founders & Product Builders** – Developing scalable, high-quality apps.

- **Computer Science Students & Self-Learners** – Wanting to specialize in mobile development.

If you struggle with app architecture, performance optimization, or advanced UI features—this book will guide you step by step.

Tools & Setup (What You'll Need)

Before coding, ensure you have these tools installed:

1. Android Studio (Latest Version)

- Download from **developer.android.com/studio**

- Supports **Java & Kotlin**

- Integrated **emulator** for testing apps

2. Device Emulator or Physical Android Phone

- **Emulator:** Comes with Android Studio.

- **Physical device:** Enable **USB debugging** under Developer Options.

3. Version Control with Git & GitHub

- Install **Git** via git-scm.com

- **GitHub** for storing and collaborating on code

4. Firebase for Cloud Features

- **Authentication:** Google, Email/Password, Social Logins.

- **Firestore Database:** Cloud-based real-time storage.

- **Cloud Messaging (FCM):** Push notifications.

5. CI/CD Pipelines for Automation

- **GitHub Actions** for automating testing & deployment.

- **Fastlane** for automating Play Store releases.

Mini Challenge: Set up a GitHub repo, push a simple Android project, and enable Firebase Authentication.

How to Use This Book Effectively

- **Follow Along with the Code Examples**

- **Try the Challenges & Exercises**

- **Apply What You Learn to Your Own Apps**

- **Engage with the Android Developer Community**

- **Stay Updated with the Latest Android Trends**

Final Words Before We Begin

By the end of this book, you will:

- Be comfortable **building modern, scalable Android apps**

- Understand **Jetpack Compose, MVVM, Firebase, AI, and CI/CD**

- Be ready to **publish and monetize apps professionally**

Are you ready to **level up** your Android development skills?

Let's get started with **Advanced UI Design & Jetpack Compose**.

SECTION 1: ADVANCED UI & DESIGN

Chapter 1: Jetpack Compose – The Future of UI Development

User interfaces (UI) are the **heart of any Android application**. They define how users interact with an app and can make or break the user experience. For years, Android developers relied on **XML layouts** combined with imperative UI programming to build interfaces. However, as apps became more complex, XML-based UI development introduced **several challenges**:

- **UI code was fragmented** between XML files and Kotlin/Java code.

- **State handling was cumbersome**, requiring ViewModels, LiveData, or manual synchronization.

- **Dynamic and reusable UI elements were difficult to implement.**

To address these issues, Google introduced **Jetpack Compose**, a modern, declarative UI framework designed to make UI development **simpler, faster, and more efficient**. In this chapter, you will learn why Jetpack Compose is the future of Android UI development and how to use its powerful features to build **beautiful, dynamic interfaces**.

1. Why Jetpack Compose Over XML?

For years, Android UI development relied on **XML layouts** and the **View-based UI system**. While functional, this approach came with **several limitations**:

1.1 The Limitations of XML-Based UI Development

1. **Separation of UI and Logic**

   o XML files define UI components, while Kotlin/Java handles logic in separate files.

   o Keeping UI and logic in sync requires **boilerplate code and additional complexity**.

2. **Manual View Binding**

   o Developers need to **find and bind views manually** using findViewById() or View Binding.

   o This makes code **longer and harder to maintain**.

3. **Difficult State Management**

o Handling UI state across multiple Views and Activities requires **LiveData, ViewModels, or custom listeners**.

o UI updates often require manually calling setText(), setVisibility(), or triggering invalidate().

4. **Performance Issues**

o XML layouts involve **hierarchical tree structures**, leading to **slower rendering**.

o Deeply nested layouts reduce **UI performance**.

1.2 The Advantages of Jetpack Compose

Jetpack Compose solves these issues by **replacing XML with a declarative UI system** built in Kotlin.

✓ **Less Boilerplate Code** – UI and logic are written in the same file, making code more **readable and maintainable**.

✓ **State-Driven UI** – UI updates automatically when state changes, reducing the need for manual findViewById().

✓ **More Performance Efficient** – Composable functions only **recompose** the UI elements that change, avoiding full UI redraws.

✓ **Reusable UI Components** – Custom UI elements are **easier to create and reuse**. ✓ **Built for Modern App Development** – Jetpack Compose integrates seamlessly with **Kotlin, Coroutines, and LiveData/Flow**.

Case Study:

Google rewrote the Play Store UI using Jetpack Compose, reducing UI development time by **30%** and improving UI performance.

2. Composable Functions & State Management

2.1 What Are Composable Functions?

Jetpack Compose is built around **Composable functions**, which **define UI elements declaratively**. Unlike XML, which defines static layouts, Composable functions allow you to build **dynamic, interactive UI components**.

Basic Composable Function Example

kotlin

```
@Composable

fun Greeting(name: String) {

    Text(text = "Hello, $name!")

}
```

- The **@Composable annotation** tells the compiler that this function **creates UI elements**.

- This function takes a parameter (name) and updates the text dynamically.

2.2 State Management in Jetpack Compose

One of the biggest advantages of Jetpack Compose is its **state-driven UI**. This means that UI elements **automatically update when data changes**, without needing manual intervention.

Using remember for State

kotlin

```kotlin
@Composable

fun Counter() {

    var count by remember { mutableStateOf(0) }


    Column {

        Text(text = "Count: $count")

        Button(onClick = { count++ }) {

            Text("Increase Count")

        }

    }

}
```

- mutableStateOf(0) creates a **state variable** (count) that holds an integer value.

- When the button is clicked, count is updated, and Jetpack Compose **automatically recomposes the UI**.

2.3 Remembering State Across Recomposition

If state is not properly managed, UI elements **reset when recomposed**. To prevent this, use remember:

kotlin

var text by remember { mutableStateOf("Hello") }

For **long-lived state** (such as data fetched from a database), use **ViewModel** and rememberSaveable.

3. Building Complex UI with LazyColumn, LazyRow, and Cards

3.1 Displaying Lists Efficiently with LazyColumn

LazyColumn is **the Jetpack Compose equivalent of RecyclerView**. It renders **large lists efficiently** by **recycling UI components** instead of recreating them.

kotlin

@Composable

```kotlin
fun NameList(names: List<String>) {

    LazyColumn {

        items(names) { name ->

            Text(text = "Hello, $name!", fontSize = 20.sp, modifier = Modifier.padding(8.dp))

        }

    }

}
```

- **LazyColumn { items(...) }** replaces RecyclerView.Adapter.

- **Only visible items are rendered**, improving performance.

3.2 Horizontal Scrolling with LazyRow

For **horizontally scrolling lists**, use LazyRow:

kotlin

@Composable

```kotlin
fun ImageGallery(images: List<Int>) {

    LazyRow {

        items(images) { imageRes ->

            Image(painter = painterResource(id = imageRes),
contentDescription = null)

        }

    }

}
```

3.3 Using Cards for Modern UI Design

Cards create **visually distinct, elegant UI elements**:

kotlin

```kotlin
@Composable

fun InfoCard(title: String, description: String) {

    Card(

        elevation = 4.dp,

        modifier = Modifier.padding(8.dp)
```

```
) {

    Column(modifier = Modifier.padding(16.dp)) {

        Text(text = title, fontWeight = FontWeight.Bold,
fontSize = 18.sp)

        Text(text = description)

    }

}

}
```

4. Animations & Transitions in Jetpack Compose

Jetpack Compose **simplifies animations** with built-in functions like animateFloatAsState.

4.1 Simple Button Animation

kotlin

@Composable

```kotlin
fun AnimatedButton() {

    var expanded by remember { mutableStateOf(false) }

    val size by animateDpAsState(targetValue = if (expanded)
200.dp else 100.dp)


    Button(

        onClick = { expanded = !expanded },

        modifier = Modifier.size(size)

    ) {

        Text("Tap Me")

    }

}
```

- Clicking the button **smoothly expands and shrinks it**.

4.2 Page Transitions Using AnimatedVisibility

kotlin

```kotlin
@Composable
```

```
fun AnimatedContent(isVisible: Boolean) {

   AnimatedVisibility(visible = isVisible) {

      Text("Now you see me!", fontSize = 24.sp)

   }

}
```

- AnimatedVisibility **fades elements in and out** dynamically.

Mini-Challenge: Build a Dynamic UI with Animations

Objective:

- Create a **list of cards** with a **"Like" button** inside each.

- When the button is clicked, **animate the card size** and **change the button color**.

Hints:

- Use LazyColumn for the list.

- Use animateColorAsState to change button color.

- Use animateDpAsState to change card size.

Chapter 2: Responsive & Adaptive UI Design

In today's digital world, Android apps run on **a vast range of devices**—from small-screen smartphones to large-screen tablets, foldable devices, and even smart TVs. As an Android developer, ensuring that your app looks and functions **consistently across different screen sizes** is **crucial for user experience and engagement**.

A **responsive and adaptive UI** dynamically adjusts to various screen sizes, orientations, and device capabilities. Beyond responsiveness, modern Android apps must also support **dark mode, custom themes, and accessibility features** to ensure usability for **all users, including those with disabilities**.

In this chapter, you will learn:

✓ How to design layouts that work across **phones, tablets, and foldables**

✓ How to implement **dark mode and custom themes**

✓ How to create **inclusive, accessible UI** following **Google's Material Design best practices**

1. Designing for Multiple Screen Sizes (Phones, Tablets, Foldables)

1.1 Understanding Screen Densities and Sizes

Android devices come in **different screen sizes and resolutions**. Instead of designing separate layouts for each device, Android provides **Density-independent Pixels (dp)** and **Scaled Pixels (sp)** to ensure layouts scale proportionally.

- **dp (Density-independent Pixels):** Used for defining layout dimensions (width, height, margins, paddings).

- **sp (Scale-independent Pixels):** Used for text sizes, ensuring readability across different screen resolutions.

1.2 Using ConstraintLayout for Responsive Design

ConstraintLayout allows **flexible positioning of UI elements** without requiring nested layouts. It adapts well to **different screen sizes and orientations**.

Example: Adaptive Layout Using ConstraintLayout

xml

<androidx.constraintlayout.widget.ConstraintLayout

```xml
xmlns:android="http://schemas.android.com/apk/res/android"

  xmlns:app="http://schemas.android.com/apk/res-auto"

  android:layout_width="match_parent"

  android:layout_height="match_parent">


  <TextView

    android:id="@+id/titleText"

    android:layout_width="0dp"

    android:layout_height="wrap_content"

    android:text="Welcome to My App"

    app:layout_constraintTop_toTopOf="parent"

    app:layout_constraintStart_toStartOf="parent"

    app:layout_constraintEnd_toEndOf="parent" />


</androidx.constraintlayout.widget.ConstraintLayout>
```

✓ Uses **0dp width** to allow flexible expansion

✓ Centers text dynamically on **all screen sizes**

1.3 Adapting to Tablets and Large Screens

On tablets, you can display **multiple content sections** side by side instead of stacking them.

Using Fragments for Adaptive Layouts

- For phones, use **single-pane layouts** (one Fragment per screen).

- For tablets, use **dual-pane layouts** (side-by-side Fragments).

Example:

xml

```xml
<!-- res/layout/activity_main.xml (For Phones) -->
<FrameLayout

    android:id="@+id/container"

    android:layout_width="match_parent"
```

```
    android:layout_height="match_parent" />
```
xml


```xml
<!-- res/layout-sw600dp/activity_main.xml (For Tablets) -->
<LinearLayout

    android:orientation="horizontal"

    android:layout_width="match_parent"

    android:layout_height="match_parent">


    <FrameLayout

        android:id="@+id/menu_container"

        android:layout_width="0dp"

        android:layout_weight="1"

        android:layout_height="match_parent"/>


    <FrameLayout

        android:id="@+id/detail_container"
```

```
android:layout_width="0dp"

android:layout_weight="2"

android:layout_height="match_parent"/>
```

</LinearLayout>

✓ Uses **sw600dp qualifier** to load a **tablet-specific layout**

✓ Displays **menu on the left, details on the right**

1.4 Designing for Foldable Devices

Foldables introduce **two-screen states**:

- **Unfolded mode** (tablet-like UI)

- **Folded mode** (compact phone UI)

Use **WindowMetrics API** to detect screen changes dynamically.

kotlin

```
val                     windowMetrics            =
WindowMetricsCalculator.getOrCreate().computeCurrentWi
ndowMetrics(activity)
```

```kotlin
val width = windowMetrics.bounds.width()
```

✓ Adapts UI when users fold/unfold their device

2. Dark Mode & Custom Themes

2.1 Why Support Dark Mode?

Dark mode is now a **standard UI feature** in Android apps, offering:

✓ Improved **battery efficiency** (especially on OLED screens)

✓ Reduced **eye strain in low-light environments**

2.2 Implementing Dark Mode in Jetpack Compose

Jetpack Compose makes it **easy to support dark mode** using MaterialTheme.

kotlin

```kotlin
@Composable

fun MyAppTheme(darkTheme: Boolean = isSystemInDarkTheme(), content: @Composable () -> Unit) {
```

```kotlin
val colors = if (darkTheme) darkColors() else lightColors()


MaterialTheme(

    colors = colors,

    typography = Typography,

    shapes = Shapes,

    content = content

)
}
```

✓ **Detects system-wide dark mode settings**

✓ **Automatically switches themes**

2.3 Customizing Themes

You can define **custom colors, typography, and shapes** in Jetpack Compose.

Example: Custom Theme Colors

kotlin

```
val LightColorPalette = lightColors(

    primary = Color(0xFF6200EA),

    background = Color.White

)

val DarkColorPalette = darkColors(

    primary = Color(0xFFBB86FC),

    background = Color.Black

)
```

✓ Allows **branded themes**

✓ Supports **light and dark variations**

3. Accessibility Best Practices for Inclusive Apps

3.1 Why Accessibility Matters

Millions of users rely on **screen readers, text magnifiers, and voice navigation** to use apps. **Google's Material Design** recommends accessibility as a **core design principle**.

3.2 Implementing Text Scaling and Contrast

Use **scaled pixels (sp)** instead of fixed sizes:

kotlin

```
Text(
    text = "Large Text",
    fontSize = 20.sp
)
```

✓ Ensures **text adapts to user settings**

Improve contrast using **high-contrast themes**:

kotlin

```
colors = darkColors(
    primary = Color(0xFFFFFF00), // High contrast yellow
    background = Color.Black
)
```

3.3 Adding Content Descriptions for Screen Readers

kotlin

```kotlin
Image(
    painter = painterResource(R.drawable.profile),
    contentDescription = "User profile picture"
)
```

✓ Allows **visually impaired users** to understand images

3.4 Touch Target Size Best Practices

Ensure buttons and interactive elements are **at least 48dp x 48dp** for usability.

kotlin

```kotlin
Button(
    modifier = Modifier.size(48.dp),
    onClick = { /* Action */ }
) {
```

```kotlin
    Text("Click Me")
}
```

✓ Prevents **accidental misclicks**

3.5 Keyboard and Navigation Support

- Use focusable(true) for keyboard navigation.

- Implement **voice control compatibility** using ActionLabels.

kotlin

```kotlin
Button(
    onClick = { /* Action */ },

    modifier = Modifier.semantics { contentDescription = "Submit Form" }
) {
    Text("Submit")
}
```

✓ Supports **voice commands and screen readers**

Pro Tip: Best Practices from Google's Material Design

Google's **Material Design** provides guidelines for:

✓ **Consistent UI across screen sizes**

✓ **Adaptive layouts with responsive grids**

✓ **Dark mode, animations, and motion design**

✓ **Inclusive, accessible user experiences**

Key Takeaways from Material Design

- Use **Material Theming** for consistent UI

- Follow **Dynamic Color Adaptation** (Material You)

- Implement **Gesture Navigation** for intuitive user interactions

- Optimize UI for **Foldables and Large Screens**

Chapter 3: Custom Views & Advanced UI Components

Modern Android applications demand **highly interactive, visually engaging, and performance-optimized user interfaces**. While Jetpack Compose and standard UI components provide **flexibility and convenience**, sometimes **predefined UI elements** are not enough.

For a truly **unique and branded user experience**, developers often need to create **custom views, implement complex animations, and fine-tune UI performance** to deliver smooth, visually appealing interfaces.

In this chapter, we will cover:

✓ How to **create custom views and animations**

✓ How to **implement gesture controls and touch interactions**

✓ How to **optimize UI performance for 60fps rendering**

✓ **A case study on Instagram's UI performance optimizations**

1. Creating Custom Views & Custom Animations

1.1 What Are Custom Views?

Custom Views are UI components that **extend default Android Views or create entirely new ones** to provide **unique behavior and styling**.

You might need a custom view when:

- You want **non-standard UI elements** (e.g., a **custom slider** or a **circular progress bar**).

- You need **highly optimized drawing performance** (e.g., custom charts or dashboards).

- You require **advanced animations or gesture support** that standard views do not provide.

1.2 Creating a Simple Custom View

Example: A Circular Progress Bar

kotlin

```kotlin
class CircularProgressView(context: Context, attrs: AttributeSet?) : View(context, attrs) {

    private val paint = Paint().apply {
        color = Color.BLUE
        strokeWidth = 15f
        style = Paint.Style.STROKE
        isAntiAlias = true
    }

    private var progress = 0f

    fun setProgress(value: Float) {
        progress = value
        invalidate() // Triggers redraw
    }
}
```

```kotlin
override fun onDraw(canvas: Canvas) {

    super.onDraw(canvas)

    val centerX = width / 2f

    val centerY = height / 2f

    val radius = min(centerX, centerY) - paint.strokeWidth

    canvas.drawArc(

        centerX - radius, centerY - radius,

        centerX + radius, centerY + radius,

        -90f, progress * 3.6f, false, paint

    )

}

}
```

Key Concepts:

✓ Uses onDraw() to render UI manually

✓ invalidate() forces UI to refresh when progress changes

✓ Paint object applies **colors, stroke width, and anti-aliasing** for smooth rendering

1.3 Custom Animations with ValueAnimator

Adding animations improves UI engagement. You can use **ValueAnimator** to animate UI elements smoothly.

Example: Animating Progress Bar

kotlin

```kotlin
val animator = ValueAnimator.ofFloat(0f, 100f).apply {

    duration = 2000

    addUpdateListener {

        setProgress(it.animatedValue as Float)

    }

    start()

}
```

✓ **Smoothly animates progress changes over 2 seconds**

✓ **Updates UI frame-by-frame** for fluid motion

2. Implementing Gesture Controls & Touch Interactions

2.1 Why Gesture Controls Matter?

Gestures **enhance user interaction** by allowing users to swipe, pinch, tap, or drag elements.

Common gestures include:

✓ **Tap** – Selecting an item

✓ **Swipe** – Navigating between screens

✓ **Pinch** – Zooming in/out

✓ **Drag & Drop** – Reordering items

2.2 Implementing Tap and Drag Gestures

Jetpack Compose provides **Modifier.pointerInput()** for handling gestures.

Example: Detecting Tap Gestures

kotlin

```kotlin
@Composable

fun TapGestureExample() {

    Box(

        modifier = Modifier

            .size(200.dp)

            .background(Color.Gray)

            .pointerInput(Unit) {

                detectTapGestures(

                    onTap = { Log.d("Gesture", "Tapped!") }

                )

            }

    )

}
```

✓ Detects **single taps** and logs them

Example: Dragging UI Elements

kotlin

```kotlin
@Composable

fun DraggableBox() {

  var offsetX by remember { mutableStateOf(0f) }


  Box(

    modifier = Modifier

      .size(100.dp)

      .offset { IntOffset(offsetX.roundToInt(), 0) }

      .background(Color.Red)

      .pointerInput(Unit) {

        detectDragGestures { change, dragAmount ->

          offsetX += dragAmount.x

        }

      }

  )
```

```
}
```

✓ Allows **dragging a red box horizontally**

2.3 Multi-Touch Gestures (Pinch to Zoom)

To implement **pinch-to-zoom**, use TransformGestureDetector.

Example: Pinch to Zoom an Image

kotlin

```
@Composable

fun ZoomableImage() {

    var scale by remember { mutableStateOf(1f) }


    Image(

        painter = painterResource(R.drawable.sample_image),

        contentDescription = null,

        modifier = Modifier
```

```
    .size(300.dp)

    .scale(scale)

    .pointerInput(Unit) {

        detectTransformGestures { _, _, zoom, _ ->

            scale *= zoom

        }

    }

)

}
```

✓ Detects **multi-touch pinch gestures** to scale images

3. Optimizing UI Performance & Smooth Rendering (60fps)

3.1 Why 60fps Matters?

A **smooth UI** runs at **60 frames per second (fps)**, ensuring animations and interactions feel **natural and fluid.**

Performance issues arise due to:

✘ **Overdraw** – When a UI element is drawn multiple times unnecessarily

✘ **Heavy UI rendering** – Complex layouts with too many nested views

✘ **Inefficient state updates** – Unnecessary recompositions in Jetpack Compose

3.2 Best Practices for Performance Optimization

✓ **Avoid Nested Layouts** – Use ConstraintLayout instead of LinearLayout nesting

✓ **Use LazyColumn Instead of RecyclerView** – Efficient rendering of lists

✓ **Minimize UI Recomposition** – Use remember to store UI states

✓ **Use Hardware Acceleration** – Ensure animations use GPU rendering

Case Study: How Instagram Optimizes UI Performance

Instagram is one of the **most visually intensive apps** with **real-time feeds, infinite scrolling, and high-resolution images**. Here's how it **optimizes UI performance**:

1. Smart Image Loading with Glide

Instagram uses **Glide**, a high-performance image loading library that:

- **Caches images in memory** to avoid re-downloading
- **Automatically resizes images** to fit screen resolution
- **Uses background threads** to load images smoothly

kotlin

```
Glide.with(context)

    .load("https://example.com/image.jpg")

    .into(imageView)
```

✓ Prevents **UI lag when scrolling feeds**

2. Efficient List Rendering

Instagram **reuses list items efficiently** using:

✓ LazyColumn (for Compose) or RecyclerView (for Views)

✓ **ViewHolder pattern** to cache and reuse UI elements

kotlin

```
LazyColumn {

    items(postList) { post ->

        PostItem(post)

    }

}
```

✓ Avoids **UI lag and excessive rendering**

3. Background Processing for Smooth Interactions

Instagram **moves heavy tasks off the main UI thread** using:

✓ **WorkManager** for scheduled background tasks

✓ **Coroutines & Kotlin Flow** for real-time updates

kotlin

```
viewModelScope.launch {

    val feedData = repository.getLatestPosts()

    _uiState.value = feedData

}
```

✓ Ensures **the UI stays responsive while loading new posts**

SECTION 2: ARCHITECTURE & PERFORMANCE OPTIMIZATION

Chapter 4: MVVM & Clean Architecture

As Android applications become more complex, managing UI logic, data handling, and business logic in a structured way becomes essential. In the early days of Android development, many apps followed the **Activity-centric approach**, where UI logic and data operations were tightly coupled within Activities and Fragments. This often led to **hard-to-maintain, error-prone, and non-scalable applications**.

To address this issue, Google introduced **MVVM (Model-View-ViewModel)**, an architectural pattern that separates UI logic from business logic, making apps **more maintainable, scalable, and testable**. Furthermore, **Clean Architecture**, introduced by Robert C. Martin, provides a **layered architecture** that ensures modularity and separation of concerns.

In this chapter, we will cover:

- Why **MVVM** is the preferred architecture for modern Android applications

- How to implement the **Repository pattern** and **ViewModels**

- The differences between **LiveData, StateFlow, and SharedFlow**

- How to use **Dependency Injection (Hilt and Dagger 2)**

- Common mistakes developers make while using **MVVM and Clean Architecture**

1. Why Use MVVM?

MVVM (**Model-View-ViewModel**) is the **recommended architecture** by Google for Android development because it provides:

1.1 Separation of Concerns

- **View (Activity/Fragment/Compose UI):** Handles UI and user interactions

- **ViewModel:** Stores and manages UI-related data and business logic

- **Model:** Manages data sources (Database, API, etc.)

This separation ensures that UI logic does not directly manipulate data, making the app **easier to test and modify**.

1.2 Benefits of MVVM

✓ **Improves code maintainability** – UI code remains separate from business logic

✓ **Simplifies testing** – ViewModels can be tested independently

✓ **Prevents memory leaks** – ViewModels survive configuration changes (e.g., screen rotation)

✓ **Enhances scalability** – Easily extendable for large applications

2. Implementing Repository Pattern & ViewModels

2.1 Repository Pattern Overview

The **Repository pattern** provides a **clean API** for managing data from multiple sources, such as a **local database and a remote API**. Instead of Activities or Fragments directly handling data, the Repository acts as a **single source of truth**.

2.2 Implementing a Repository

Step 1: Create a Data Model

kotlin

```
data class User(
    val id: Int,
```

```kotlin
    val name: String,

    val email: String
)
```

Step 2: Create a DAO for Local Database Operations

kotlin

```kotlin
@Dao
interface UserDao {
    @Query("SELECT * FROM users")
    fun getAllUsers(): LiveData<List<User>>

    @Insert(onConflict = OnConflictStrategy.REPLACE)
    suspend fun insertUser(user: User)
}
```

Step 3: Implement the Repository

kotlin

```kotlin
class UserRepository(private val userDao: UserDao, private
val apiService: ApiService) {

    fun getUsers(): LiveData<List<User>> {

        return userDao.getAllUsers()

    }


    suspend fun fetchUsersFromApi() {

        val response = apiService.getUsers()

        response.body()?.let { users ->

            userDao.insertUser(users)

        }

    }

}
```

2.3 Creating a ViewModel

The **ViewModel** fetches data from the repository and exposes it to the UI.

kotlin

```kotlin
class UserViewModel(private val repository: UserRepository)
: ViewModel() {

    val users: LiveData<List<User>> = repository.getUsers()

    fun fetchUsers() {
        viewModelScope.launch {
            repository.fetchUsersFromApi()
        }
    }
}
```

✓ Uses **LiveData** to observe changes

✓ Uses **Coroutines** to fetch data asynchronously

3. LiveData vs StateFlow vs SharedFlow

3.1 What is LiveData?

LiveData is a lifecycle-aware data holder that allows **automatic UI updates** when data changes.

Example Usage:

kotlin

```
val users: LiveData<List<User>> = repository.getUsers()

users.observe(viewLifecycleOwner) { userList ->

    updateUI(userList)

}
```

✓ **Automatically handles lifecycle events**

✓ **UI updates only when Active**

3.2 What is StateFlow?

StateFlow is part of Kotlin's Flow API and is used to **store and manage UI state in ViewModels**.

Example Usage:

kotlin

```kotlin
private val _userStateFlow = MutableStateFlow<List<User>>(emptyList())

val userStateFlow: StateFlow<List<User>> = _userStateFlow


fun fetchUsers() {

    viewModelScope.launch {

        val users = repository.getUsers()

        _userStateFlow.value = users

    }

}
```

✓ **Always holds the latest value**

✓ **Recommended for UI state management**

3.3 What is SharedFlow?

SharedFlow is similar to **LiveData**, but it is **hot** and supports multiple collectors.

Example Usage:

kotlin

```
private val _eventFlow = MutableSharedFlow<String>()

val eventFlow = _eventFlow.asSharedFlow()


fun sendEvent(message: String) {

  viewModelScope.launch {

    _eventFlow.emit(message)

  }

}
```

✓ Ideal for **one-time events** like **toasts and navigation actions**

4. Using Dependency Injection (Hilt, Dagger 2)

4.1 Why Use Dependency Injection?

Dependency Injection (DI) improves code **modularity, testability, and scalability** by injecting dependencies instead of creating them manually.

4.2 Implementing Hilt for DI

Step 1: Add Dependencies to build.gradle

gradle

```
dependencies {
    implementation "com.google.dagger:hilt-android:2.44"
    kapt "com.google.dagger:hilt-compiler:2.44"
}
```

Step 2: Enable Hilt in Application Class

kotlin

```kotlin
@HiltAndroidApp

class MyApplication : Application()
```

Step 3: Provide Dependencies with Hilt Modules

kotlin

```kotlin
@Module

@InstallIn(SingletonComponent::class)

object AppModule {

    @Provides

    fun provideApiService(): ApiService {

        return Retrofit.Builder()

            .baseUrl("https://example.com/")

            .addConverterFactory(GsonConverterFactory.create())

            .build()

            .create(ApiService::class.java)
```

```
    }

}
```

✓ Provides **a single instance of dependencies** throughout the app

4.3 Using Dagger 2 for Manual Dependency Injection

If you need **more control**, you can use **Dagger 2**, but it requires more boilerplate code than Hilt.

Example:

kotlin

```
@Component(modules = [NetworkModule::class])

interface AppComponent {

    fun inject(activity: MainActivity)

}
```

✓ Suitable for **large-scale applications** with complex dependencies

Expert Insight: Common MVVM Mistakes

1. **Overloading ViewModels**

   o **Mistake:** Placing too much logic in ViewModels

   o **Solution:** Move data-fetching logic to Repositories

2. **Not Handling Lifecycle Properly**

   o **Mistake:** Observing LiveData in Fragments without clearing references

   o **Solution:** Use viewLifecycleOwner.lifecycleScope

3. **Overusing MutableLiveData**

   o **Mistake:** Exposing MutableLiveData to UI

   o **Solution:** Use LiveData for UI and keep MutableLiveData private

4. **Not Using Dependency Injection**

   o **Mistake:** Creating dependencies inside ViewModels

- **Solution:** Inject dependencies using Hilt/Dagger

Chapter 5: Improving Performance & Reducing App Size

Performance optimization is a **critical aspect** of Android development. A slow or unresponsive app leads to **poor user experience, high battery consumption, and increased uninstall rates**. In addition, **large APK sizes** increase **app download time and storage usage**, discouraging users from installing or keeping the app.

This chapter will guide you through essential **performance optimization techniques** to ensure your Android apps are **fast, responsive, and lightweight**. We will cover:

- **Profiling & Debugging with Android Studio** to identify bottlenecks

- **Fixing ANR (App Not Responding) issues** to prevent app crashes

- **Reducing APK size using ProGuard & R8** for better storage efficiency

- **Using Jetpack WorkManager for background processing** to improve responsiveness

- **A checklist of best practices** to ensure optimal performance

By applying these techniques, you will create **efficient, optimized, and smooth-performing applications**.

1. Profiling & Debugging with Android Studio

1.1 Why Profiling is Important

Profiling helps **analyze app performance** by detecting:

✓ **Slow UI rendering** causing laggy animations

✓ **High memory usage** leading to OutOfMemory (OOM) crashes

✓ **Excessive CPU or network activity** draining battery

1.2 Using Android Studio Profiler

Android Studio provides **built-in profiling tools** to monitor:

- **CPU usage** (to detect slow processing)

- **Memory leaks** (to identify inefficient memory usage)

- **Network requests** (to track API call delays)

Step 1: Open the Profiler

1. Run your app in **Debug mode**.

2. Navigate to **View → Tool Windows → Profiler**.

3. Select your app and click **CPU, Memory, or Network** profiling tabs.

Step 2: Analyze CPU Performance

- Look for **high CPU spikes** that indicate inefficient background processing.

- Identify **long-running operations** blocking the UI thread.

Step 3: Detect Memory Leaks

- Use **Heap Dump Analysis** to check objects that are **not released after use**.

- Enable **Garbage Collection (GC) logs** to analyze memory deallocation.

Step 4: Optimize Network Calls

- Use **Network Profiler** to monitor API response times.

- Reduce **unnecessary API requests** and enable **caching** for frequently used data.

Pro Tip: Always test performance on **real devices** as emulators do not accurately reflect real-world usage.

2. Fixing ANR (App Not Responding) Issues

2.1 What Causes ANR Errors?

An ANR occurs when an app **fails to respond within 5 seconds** to user input. Common causes include:

✘ **Blocking the main UI thread** with heavy operations

✘ **Slow database queries or API calls** running on the main thread

✘ **Too many nested views** causing rendering delays

2.2 Detecting ANR Issues

Android provides **ANR reports** in adb logs.

Check ANR logs using ADB

sh

adb shell dumpsys activity anr

2.3 Best Practices to Prevent ANRs

Run Heavy Tasks in Background Threads

Use **Coroutines or Executors** to perform **network calls, database queries, or file operations** in the background.

kotlin

```kotlin
viewModelScope.launch(Dispatchers.IO) {

    val users = database.getUsers()

    withContext(Dispatchers.Main) {

        updateUI(users)

    }

}
```

✓ Moves heavy database calls to **IO thread**, preventing UI freeze

Use Handlers for Delayed UI Updates

kotlin

```kotlin
Handler(Looper.getMainLooper()).postDelayed({

    textView.text = "Updated after 3 seconds"

}, 3000)
```

✓ Ensures **delayed operations do not block UI interactions**

Optimize RecyclerView Performance

- Use setHasFixedSize(true) to **improve list rendering speed**.

- Use DiffUtil for **efficient list updates**.

kotlin

recyclerView.setHasFixedSize(true)

✓ Reduces **layout recalculations** for lists

3. Reducing APK Size with ProGuard & R8

3.1 Why Reduce APK Size?

Large APKs increase:

✗ **App download time**

✗ **Storage consumption**

✗ **User uninstall rates**

3.2 How ProGuard & R8 Work

What is ProGuard?

ProGuard is a **code shrinker and obfuscator** that:

✓ **Removes unused classes and methods**

✓ **Shrinks resource files**

✓ **Obfuscates code to prevent reverse engineering**

What is R8?

R8 is the **replacement for ProGuard**, providing:

✓ **Better performance** (faster builds)

✓ **Smaller APK sizes**

✓ **Improved obfuscation**

3.3 Enabling R8 in Gradle

gradle

```
android {
    buildTypes {
        release {
            minifyEnabled true
```

```
            proguardFiles        getDefaultProguardFile('proguard-
android-optimize.txt'), 'proguard-rules.pro'

        }

    }

}
```

✓ **Minifies and obfuscates code in release builds**

3.4 Removing Unused Resources

Enable **resource shrinking** in gradle.properties:

gradle

```
android {

    buildTypes {

        release {

            shrinkResources true

        }

    }

}
```

✓ Removes **unused images, layouts, and strings**

3.5 Compressing Image Assets

Use **WebP format** instead of PNG/JPEG to **reduce image sizes** without losing quality.

✓ Convert PNGs to WebP in **Android Studio** → **Right-click** → **Convert to WebP**

4. Background Processing with Jetpack WorkManager

4.1 Why Use WorkManager?

WorkManager is **the recommended API** for background tasks that:

- Must run even after app restarts

- Require scheduling (e.g., syncing data, sending notifications)

4.2 Implementing WorkManager

Step 1: Add WorkManager Dependency

gradle

```
dependencies {

    implementation "androidx.work:work-runtime:2.7.1"

}
```

Step 2: Create a Worker Class

kotlin

```kotlin
class SyncWorker(context: Context, workerParams:
WorkerParameters) : Worker(context, workerParams) {

    override fun doWork(): Result {

        syncDataFromServer()

        return Result.success()

    }

}
```

Step 3: Schedule Background Work

kotlin

```kotlin
val                    workRequest                    =
PeriodicWorkRequestBuilder<SyncWorker>(15,
TimeUnit.MINUTES).build()

WorkManager.getInstance(context).enqueue(workRequest)
```

✓ Ensures **data sync happens every 15 minutes**

Checklist: Performance Optimization Best Practices

✅ **UI Performance Optimization**

- Use ConstraintLayout instead of nested LinearLayouts

- Reduce **unnecessary UI recomposition** in Jetpack Compose

- Enable **hardware acceleration**

✅ **Fixing ANR Issues**

- Never run **network/database operations on the main thread**

- Optimize **RecyclerView performance** with setHasFixedSize(true)

- Use **asynchronous background tasks** for file processing

✅ Reducing APK Size

- Enable **ProGuard and R8**

- Convert **PNG/JPEG images to WebP**

- Enable **resource shrinking**

✅ Background Processing

- Use **WorkManager** for scheduled tasks

- Use **Coroutines for background operations**

By following these **best practices**, your app will:

✓ Load **faster**

✓ Consume **less memory**

✓ Deliver **a smooth and responsive experience**

SECTION 3: NETWORKING & DATA MANAGEMENT

Chapter 6: Advanced Networking: REST, GraphQL, & WebSockets

Networking is a **critical part** of modern Android applications. Most apps rely on APIs to fetch and send data, enabling users to interact with cloud-based services, databases, or real-time updates.

For years, **REST (Representational State Transfer)** has been the standard for web services. However, with increasing demand for **more efficient and flexible data fetching**, **GraphQL** has emerged as an alternative. In addition, **WebSockets** provide real-time two-way communication, making them essential for applications like messaging, gaming, and financial trading.

This chapter will cover:

- **REST vs GraphQL** – Understanding when to use each

- **Making API calls efficiently with Retrofit**

- **Implementing WebSockets for real-time data updates**

- **Using OAuth & JWT for secure authentication**

- **A case study on how TikTok handles real-time data**

By the end of this chapter, you will be able to build **fast, scalable, and secure networking features in your Android applications**.

1. REST vs GraphQL: When to Use Each?

1.1 Understanding REST (Representational State Transfer)

REST is a **widely used web architecture** based on HTTP requests and responses.

Key Features of REST:

✓ Uses standard HTTP methods (GET, POST, PUT, DELETE)

✓ Stateless communication (each request is independent)

✓ Returns JSON/XML responses

Example REST API Request (Fetching User Data):

http

GET /users/123

Host: api.example.com

Authorization: Bearer token123

Response:

json

{

  "id": 123,

  "name": "John Doe",

  "email": "johndoe@example.com"

}

1.2 Understanding GraphQL

GraphQL is an alternative API approach where **clients request only the specific data they need**.

Key Features of GraphQL:

✓ Fetches multiple resources in **a single request**

✓ Allows **custom queries** instead of fixed endpoints

✓ Prevents **over-fetching and under-fetching of data**

Example GraphQL Query (Fetching User Data):

graphql

```
{
  user(id: 123) {
    name
    email
    profilePicture
  }
}
```

Response:

json

```json
{
  "user": {
    "name": "John Doe",
    "email": "johndoe@example.com",
    "profilePicture": "https://example.com/avatar.jpg"
  }
```

}

1.3 When to Use REST vs GraphQL?

Feature	REST	GraphQL
Data Fetching	Fixed endpoints, predefined responses	Clients request only the needed fields
Efficiency	May over-fetch data	Optimized queries prevent unnecessary data
Performance	Requires multiple requests for related data	One request can retrieve related data
Best For	Simple APIs with predictable responses	Complex APIs needing flexible data retrieval

Use REST when:

- Your app requires **simple, well-defined endpoints**

- Caching and CDN support are essential

Use GraphQL when:

- Your app needs **dynamic and customizable queries**

- You want to **reduce API request payload size**

2. Retrofit & Best Practices for API Calls

2.1 What is Retrofit?

Retrofit is **the most popular HTTP client for Android**. It simplifies network requests by converting JSON responses into Kotlin objects.

2.2 Setting Up Retrofit

Step 1: Add Dependencies

gradle

```
dependencies {

    implementation 'com.squareup.retrofit2:retrofit:2.9.0'

    implementation         'com.squareup.retrofit2:converter-gson:2.9.0'

}
```

Step 2: Create a Data Model

kotlin

data class User(

    val id: Int,

    val name: String,

    val email: String

)

Step 3: Define API Interface

kotlin

```
interface ApiService {

    @GET("users/{id}")

    suspend fun getUser(@Path("id") userId: Int): Response<User>

}
```

Step 4: Implement Retrofit Client

kotlin

```kotlin
object RetrofitClient {

    private val retrofit = Retrofit.Builder()

        .baseUrl("https://api.example.com/")

        .addConverterFactory(GsonConverterFactory.create())

        .build()


    val apiService: ApiService =
    retrofit.create(ApiService::class.java)

}
```

2.3 Handling API Responses Properly

Use **safe API calls** to handle failures.

kotlin

```kotlin
suspend fun fetchUserData(userId: Int): User? {

    return try {
```

```
    val response = RetrofitClient.apiService.getUser(userId)

    if (response.isSuccessful) response.body() else null

} catch (e: Exception) {

    null

}

}
```

✓ Prevents app crashes from **network failures**

✓ Uses **try-catch to handle exceptions gracefully**

3. WebSockets for Real-Time Data Updates

3.1 What Are WebSockets?

WebSockets provide **bidirectional communication** between a client and server, making them ideal for **chat apps, stock prices, and live notifications**.

REST vs WebSockets:

Feature	REST	WebSockets

Communication	One request, one response	Continuous real-time connection
Best For	Fetching data periodically	Live updates and streaming data

3.2 Implementing WebSockets in Android

Step 1: Add Dependency

gradle

```
dependencies {
    implementation 'org.java-websocket:Java-WebSocket:1.5.2'
}
```

Step 2: Create a WebSocket Client

kotlin

```
class WebSocketManager(url: String) :
WebSocketClient(URI(url)) {
    override fun onOpen(handshakedata: ServerHandshake?) {
```

```kotlin
        Log.d("WebSocket", "Connected")

    }


    override fun onMessage(message: String?) {

        Log.d("WebSocket", "Received: $message")

    }


    override fun onClose(code: Int, reason: String?, remote: Boolean) {

        Log.d("WebSocket", "Closed: $reason")

    }


    override fun onError(ex: Exception?) {

        Log.e("WebSocket", "Error: ${ex?.message}")

    }

}
```

Step 3: Connect to a WebSocket Server

kotlin

```kotlin
val socket = WebSocketManager("wss://example.com/socket")
socket.connect()
```

✓ Enables **real-time communication** with a server

✓ Reduces **latency for live updates**

4. Secure Authentication with OAuth & JWT

4.1 What is OAuth 2.0?

OAuth is a **token-based authentication framework** used for secure API access.

Example OAuth Flow:

1. User logs in via Google/Facebook

2. The app receives an **OAuth access token**

3. The token is sent with API requests to authenticate

4.2 Using JWT (JSON Web Tokens) for Secure Authentication

JWT is a **compact, self-contained token** for secure user authentication.

Example JWT Token Format:

json

```json
{
  "sub": "123456789",
  "name": "John Doe",
  "iat": 1516239022
}
```

Example API Request with JWT:

http

```http
GET /protected-resource
Authorization: Bearer jwt_token_here
```

✓ Ensures **secure authentication and prevents session hijacking**

Case Study: How TikTok Handles Real-Time Data

1. Efficient Video Streaming

- TikTok uses **adaptive bitrate streaming** to **optimize video quality** based on network speed.

2. Real-Time WebSocket Communication

- **Live comments and likes** are updated instantly using WebSockets.

3. Edge Computing for Low Latency

- TikTok caches content **closer to users** to reduce load times.

Chapter 7: Local Data Storage & Offline-First Apps

Many modern apps rely on **data persistence** to store and retrieve information even when a device is offline. Users expect seamless experiences where data remains accessible regardless of their internet connection. This is where **local storage solutions** like **Room Database, Firebase Firestore, and encrypted storage mechanisms** come into play.

An **offline-first approach** ensures that apps remain **functional without internet access** by:

- Storing user data locally

- Synchronizing with a cloud database when online

- Providing **secure storage** to protect sensitive information

This chapter will cover:

✓ **Room Database advanced features** (migrations, transactions)

✓ **LiveData & Flow integration with Room**

✓ **Using Firebase Firestore for real-time syncing**

✓ **Securing stored data with AES and Keystore API**

✓ **Mini-challenge: Building an offline note-taking app**

By the end of this chapter, you'll be able to implement **efficient, secure, and real-time local storage solutions** for your Android applications.

1. Room Database Advanced Features (Migrations, Transactions)

1.1 What is Room Database?

Room is **Google's official ORM (Object Relational Mapping) library** for handling SQLite databases in Android. It simplifies database operations by providing:

✓ **Compile-time verification of queries**

✓ **Automatic database migration handling**

✓ **Integration with Kotlin Coroutines and Flow**

'

1.2 Setting Up Room in Your Project

Step 1: Add Dependencies

gradle

```
dependencies {
    implementation "androidx.room:room-runtime:2.5.0"
    kapt "androidx.room:room-compiler:2.5.0"
    implementation "androidx.room:room-ktx:2.5.0"
}
```

Step 2: Create a Data Entity

kotlin

```
@Entity(tableName = "notes")
data class Note(
    @PrimaryKey(autoGenerate = true) val id: Int = 0,
    val title: String,
    val content: String,
```

```kotlin
val timestamp: Long
)
```

Step 3: Define the DAO (Data Access Object)

kotlin

```kotlin
@Dao
interface NoteDao {
    @Query("SELECT * FROM notes ORDER BY timestamp DESC")
    fun getAllNotes(): LiveData<List<Note>>

    @Insert(onConflict = OnConflictStrategy.REPLACE)
    suspend fun insertNote(note: Note)

    @Delete
    suspend fun deleteNote(note: Note)
}
```

Step 4: Initialize Room Database

kotlin

```kotlin
@Database(entities = [Note::class], version = 1)
abstract class NoteDatabase : RoomDatabase() {
    abstract fun noteDao(): NoteDao
}
```

1.3 Handling Database Migrations

When modifying the database schema (e.g., adding a new column), we need to **migrate** without deleting existing data.

Step 1: Modify the Entity

kotlin

```kotlin
@Entity(tableName = "notes")
data class Note(
    @PrimaryKey(autoGenerate = true) val id: Int = 0,
```

val title: String,

val content: String,

val timestamp: Long,

val category: String // New column added

)

Step 2: Define a Migration Strategy

kotlin

```kotlin
val MIGRATION_1_2 = object : Migration(1, 2) {
    override fun migrate(database: SupportSQLiteDatabase) {
        database.execSQL("ALTER TABLE notes ADD COLUMN category TEXT DEFAULT 'Uncategorized'")
    }
}
```

Step 3: Apply Migration in Database Initialization

kotlin

```kotlin
val        db        =        Room.databaseBuilder(context,
NoteDatabase::class.java, "notes.db")

    .addMigrations(MIGRATION_1_2)

    .build()
```

✓ Ensures **data integrity** while updating database schema

1.4 Using Transactions for Atomic Operations

Room supports transactions to ensure **data consistency** when performing multiple operations.

kotlin

```kotlin
@Transaction

suspend    fun    insertAndDelete(noteToDelete:    Note,
noteToInsert: Note) {

    noteDao().deleteNote(noteToDelete)

    noteDao().insertNote(noteToInsert)

}
```

✓ Ensures **either all operations succeed or none**

2. LiveData & Flow with Room

2.1 Using LiveData with Room

Room integrates seamlessly with LiveData to automatically update UI when data changes.

kotlin

```
val allNotes: LiveData<List<Note>> = noteDao.getAllNotes()

allNotes.observe(viewLifecycleOwner) { notes ->

    updateUI(notes)

}
```

✓ Ensures **real-time UI updates without manual refreshes**

2.2 Using Kotlin Flow for Asynchronous Queries

Kotlin Flow provides a more **flexible and coroutine-friendly** alternative to LiveData.

kotlin

```kotlin
@Query("SELECT * FROM notes ORDER BY timestamp DESC")
fun getAllNotesFlow(): Flow<List<Note>>
```

Observing Flow in ViewModel

kotlin

```kotlin
val allNotesFlow: StateFlow<List<Note>> = noteDao.getAllNotesFlow().stateIn(viewModelScope)
```

✓ Reduces **memory leaks and improves efficiency**

3. Firebase Firestore for Real-Time Syncing

3.1 Why Use Firestore?

Firestore is Google's real-time NoSQL cloud database. It provides:

✓ **Automatic syncing** across devices

✓ **Offline persistence** with local caching

✓ **Security rules to protect user data**

3.2 Setting Up Firestore

Step 1: Add Dependencies

gradle

```
dependencies {

    implementation    "com.google.firebase:firebase-firestore-
ktx:24.1.0"

}
```

Step 2: Initialize Firestore

kotlin

```kotlin
val db = Firebase.firestore
```

Step 3: Add Data to Firestore

kotlin

```kotlin
val note = hashMapOf(
    "title" to "My First Note",
    "content" to "This is a sample note",
    "timestamp" to System.currentTimeMillis()
)


db.collection("notes").add(note)
```

✓ Stores data in the cloud and syncs across devices

4. Secure Encrypted Storage (AES, Keystore API)

4.1 Why Secure Local Storage?

Sensitive user data (passwords, tokens) should **never** be stored in plain text. Use:

- **AES Encryption** for **secure local storage**
- **Android Keystore API** for **storing cryptographic keys**

4.2 Encrypting Data with AES

kotlin

```kotlin
fun encryptData(data: String, secretKey: SecretKey): ByteArray {
    val cipher = Cipher.getInstance("AES/GCM/NoPadding")
    cipher.init(Cipher.ENCRYPT_MODE, secretKey)
    return cipher.doFinal(data.toByteArray(Charsets.UTF_8))
}
```

✓ Ensures **data is encrypted before storage**

4.3 Storing Secure Keys with Keystore API

kotlin

```kotlin
fun generateSecretKey(): SecretKey {

    val keyGenerator =
KeyGenerator.getInstance(KeyProperties.KEY_ALGORITH
M_AES, "AndroidKeyStore")

    keyGenerator.init(KeyGenParameterSpec.Builder(

        "MySecretKey",

        KeyProperties.PURPOSE_ENCRYPT or
KeyProperties.PURPOSE_DECRYPT

    ).setBlockModes(KeyProperties.BLOCK_MODE_GCM)

.setEncryptionPaddings(KeyProperties.ENCRYPTION_PAD
DING_NONE)

    .build())

    return keyGenerator.generateKey()
}
```

✓ Prevents **key theft by storing it securely**

Mini-Challenge: Build an Offline Note-Taking App

Requirements:

✓ Users should be able to **create, edit, and delete notes**

✓ Notes should be stored **locally using Room**

✓ When online, notes should **sync with Firestore**

✓ Notes should be **securely encrypted**

Key Implementation Steps:

1. **Create Room Database** for local storage

2. **Use WorkManager** to sync notes when online

3. **Implement AES encryption** for secure storage

This challenge will **reinforce offline-first development principles** while ensuring **secure data storage and real-time synchronization**.

SECTION 4: SECURITY, TESTING, & AUTOMATION

Chapter 8: Securing Android Apps

As Android apps become more sophisticated, **securing sensitive data** and **protecting your app from malicious attacks** is more important than ever. Whether you're storing **user information**, using **API keys**, or handling **user authentication**, your app needs to **mitigate security risks**.

Hackers are constantly looking for vulnerabilities in apps to **steal sensitive data** or **reverse-engineer code**. This chapter will explore best practices to ensure your app is **secure against these threats**. We will cover:

- **ProGuard, R8, and Code Obfuscation** to protect your code from reverse engineering

- **Biometric Authentication** (Face ID, Fingerprint) to enhance security

- **Preventing API Key leaks and reverse engineering** to safeguard API access

- **Root Detection & Anti-Tampering Measures** to prevent app manipulation

- **Expert Insight: How hackers attack Android apps**

By following these security practices, you will ensure that your Android app remains **safe from external threats** and **secure for your users**.

1. ProGuard, R8, and Code Obfuscation

1.1 What is Code Obfuscation?

Code obfuscation is a technique used to **make your code difficult to understand** and reverse-engineer. It **renames classes, methods, and variables** to meaningless names, which makes it harder for attackers to understand your app's logic.

Obfuscation provides several benefits:

✓ **Prevents reverse engineering** of your app's source code

✓ **Hides sensitive code** such as API endpoints or encryption methods

✓ **Protects intellectual property**

Android supports code obfuscation via **ProGuard** and **R8**, which are **tools for code shrinking and optimization**. R8 is **the default** for newer Android projects, while ProGuard is **legacy**.

1.2 Enabling ProGuard/R8 in Your Project

To enable ProGuard or R8, you need to configure your **build.gradle** file. R8 is enabled by default in release builds, but you can configure ProGuard for extra customization.

Step 1: Enable R8/ProGuard in build.gradle

gradle

```
android {
  buildTypes {
    release {
      minifyEnabled true // Enables code shrinking
      shrinkResources true // Removes unused resources
      proguardFiles        getDefaultProguardFile('proguard-android-optimize.txt'), 'proguard-rules.pro'
    }
  }
}
```

✓ **minifyEnabled true** activates ProGuard/R8

✓ **shrinkResources true** reduces unused resources (like images or layout files)

Step 2: Create ProGuard Rules

In your **proguard-rules.pro** file, add rules for keeping classes or methods that you don't want obfuscated. For instance, you might want to keep public APIs and specific methods intact.

pro

Keep Retrofit API interfaces

-keep interface com.example.api.*

Don't obfuscate the class used for Firebase authentication

-keep class com.google.firebase.auth.FirebaseAuth { *; }

1.3 How ProGuard and R8 Protect Your Code

- **Minifies** your code by removing unused classes and methods

- **Shrinks** the code by removing unnecessary or redundant code

- **Obfuscates** class, method, and field names to **make reverse engineering difficult**

For example:

java

```java
public class ApiService {

    public String getUserData(String userId) {

        // API request code

    }

}
```

After Obfuscation:

java

```java
public class A {

    public String a(String b) {

        // API request code

    }

}
```

2. Biometric Authentication (Face ID, Fingerprint)

2.1 Why Use Biometric Authentication?

Biometric authentication offers a **higher level of security** by using **fingerprints, facial recognition**, or other biometrics instead of traditional passwords. It ensures **ease of use** while maintaining **secure user authentication**.

Benefits of Biometric Authentication:

✓ **Convenience** – Users don't need to remember passwords or PINs

✓ **Security** – Biometric data is harder to hack or steal compared to passwords

✓ **Anti-theft** – Prevents unauthorized access to the device in case of theft

2.2 Implementing Biometric Authentication in Android

Step 1: Add the Necessary Dependencies

gradle

```
dependencies {

    implementation "androidx.biometric:biometric:1.1.0"

}
```

Step 2: Check for Biometric Availability

Before implementing biometric authentication, ensure that the device **supports biometrics**.

kotlin

```kotlin
val biometricManager = BiometricManager.from(context)

val canAuthenticate = biometricManager.canAuthenticate()
```

Step 3: Trigger Biometric Authentication

kotlin

```kotlin
val executor = ContextCompat.getMainExecutor(context)

val biometricPrompt = BiometricPrompt(this, executor, object
: BiometricPrompt.AuthenticationCallback() {
```

```kotlin
    override    fun    onAuthenticationSucceeded(result:
BiometricPrompt.AuthenticationResult) {

        // Success handling

    }


    override fun onAuthenticationFailed() {

        // Failure handling

    }
})


val promptInfo = BiometricPrompt.PromptInfo.Builder()

    .setTitle("Biometric Authentication")

    .setNegativeButtonText("Use Password")

    .build()


biometricPrompt.authenticate(promptInfo)
```

Step 4: Handle Authentication Responses

- **onAuthenticationSucceeded** – The user successfully authenticated with biometrics.

- **onAuthenticationFailed** – The authentication attempt failed (incorrect fingerprint or face).

3. Preventing API Key Leaks & Reverse Engineering

3.1 Why API Key Security Matters

API keys are essential for **authenticating your app with external services**, such as Firebase, Google Maps, or third-party APIs. If attackers gain access to your API keys, they can **use your services**, rack up **charges**, or access **sensitive user data**.

3.2 How API Keys Are Leaked

API keys are often stored in the **source code** or in **configuration files** (like build.gradle or strings.xml), making them easily accessible for attackers.

3.3 Preventing API Key Leaks

1. Use Remote Configuration

Instead of embedding API keys in the app, use **remote configuration** services like **Firebase Remote Config** to load sensitive keys at runtime.

kotlin

```
FirebaseRemoteConfig.getInstance().getString("api_key")
```

2. Use Environment Variables

For local testing, store API keys in **environment variables** instead of hard-coding them in your app.

3. Encrypt API Keys

Store API keys securely by **encrypting them** in the app using the **Keystore API**. You can store them in a secure vault and decrypt them at runtime when necessary.

kotlin

```
val encryptedKey = encryptData(apiKey)
```

3.4 Code Obfuscation to Protect API Keys

Use **ProGuard** to obfuscate the code and make it harder to extract API keys. While this does not entirely prevent key extraction, it **adds an extra layer of security**.

pro

Keep encryption keys from being obfuscated

-keep class com.example.app.Encryption { *; }

4. Root Detection & Anti-Tampering Measures

4.1 Why Root Detection?

Rooting is a process by which users gain full control over their Android device, bypassing **Android's built-in security mechanisms**. Rooted devices are **more vulnerable** to malicious apps and can **bypass app security features**.

4.2 Detecting Rooted Devices

To prevent app tampering, you should detect whether the device is **rooted** and prevent sensitive operations or data access on these devices.

kotlin

```kotlin
fun isDeviceRooted(): Boolean {

    val buildTags = android.os.Build.TAGS

    val testKeys = "test-keys"

    return buildTags != null && buildTags.contains(testKeys)

}
```

4.3 Anti-Tampering Measures

1. Checking for Modified System Files

Rooted devices often have **modified system files**. Check for unusual modifications in system directories.

kotlin

```kotlin
fun checkForModifiedFiles(): Boolean {

    val path = "/system/app/Superuser.apk"

    return File(path).exists()

}
```

2. Use SafetyNet API

Google's **SafetyNet** API provides advanced checks to determine whether the device has been tampered with or rooted. It uses **Google's trusted environment** to detect and block rooted devices.

kotlin

```kotlin
val safetyNetClient = SafetyNet.getClient(this)

val task = safetyNetClient.attest(nonce, API_KEY)

task.addOnSuccessListener { response ->

    val result = response.jwsResult

}
```

5. Expert Insight: How Hackers Attack Android Apps

5.1 Common Attack Vectors

1. **Reverse Engineering**

- Attackers use **decompilers** (e.g., JADX) to analyze and modify the source code of apps, extracting sensitive information like **API keys** or **user data**.

- **Obfuscation** and **encryption** can help defend against this.

2. **Man-in-the-Middle Attacks (MITM)**

   - Attackers intercept **network traffic** to steal sensitive data, such as **API keys or authentication tokens**.

   - **SSL Pinning** can mitigate MITM attacks by **validating the server certificate**.

3. **Rooted Devices**

   - Rooting allows attackers to bypass Android's security mechanisms and tamper with the app's logic.

   - **Root detection** and **anti-tampering** measures can prevent these attacks.

4. **Code Injection & DLL Injection**

o Hackers inject **malicious code** into the app or replace native libraries to gain control of the app's behavior.

o **Integrity checks** can ensure the app's code is not tampered with or replaced.

5. **API Key Theft**

o Attackers may reverse engineer your app and extract **API keys** that are hardcoded in the source code. They can use these keys to access your backend services.

o **Encryption, remote configuration**, and **code obfuscation** significantly reduce the risk of API key theft.

5.2 Mitigating Hacker Attacks

To defend against the common types of attacks discussed above, it's important to implement a **multi-layered security strategy**. Here are some effective mitigation techniques:

1. **Encrypt Sensitive Data**

- Encrypt **API keys, tokens**, and **user data** before storing them in local storage or transmitting them over the network.

- Use the **Android Keystore API** for securely storing encryption keys.

2. **Use Strong Authentication**

- Use **multi-factor authentication (MFA)** and **biometric authentication** (Face ID, Fingerprint) for sensitive operations, ensuring unauthorized users cannot gain access.

3. **Obfuscate and Minimize Code**

- Use **ProGuard/R8** to obfuscate your app's code, making it more difficult for attackers to reverse engineer it. This reduces the ability to understand the app's internals or extract sensitive information from the code.

- **Minify the app** to remove unnecessary resources and shrink the APK size, which reduces the attack surface.

4. **Use SSL Pinning**

- SSL pinning ensures that your app can only communicate with the **legitimate backend server**. This prevents MITM attacks where hackers intercept unencrypted traffic.

- It involves storing the server's certificate or public key in the app and validating it before making secure connections.

5. **Detect Rooted Devices and Tampering**

- Implement **root detection** and check for **modified system files** or suspicious apps (e.g., Superuser.apk) on the device. If a device is rooted, you can block access or reduce functionality for security purposes.

- Use **SafetyNet Attestation API** to check whether the device has been tampered with or is running in an unsafe environment.

6. **Limit API Access**

- Apply **rate-limiting** and **throttling** to your APIs to prevent abuse.

o Implement **authentication and authorization** for every API call. Use **OAuth 2.0** and **JWT tokens** to ensure that only authorized users can access certain resources.

7. **Use Secure Coding Practices**

   o Always sanitize user inputs to prevent **SQL injection** and **cross-site scripting (XSS)**.

   o Use Android's **StrictMode** to catch accidental disk or network access on the main thread, which could slow down the app and open it to attack.

8. **Regularly Update and Patch the App**

   o Keep the app updated to address any newly discovered vulnerabilities.

   o Ensure you apply patches to any third-party libraries or dependencies that may have security issues.

Chapter 9: Automated Testing: Unit & UI Testing

As your Android applications become more complex, the need for **reliable, automated testing** grows. Automated tests allow you to ensure that your app functions as expected without manual intervention. They help identify bugs early, improve code quality, and reduce the effort needed for regression testing.

In this chapter, we will explore **unit testing, UI testing, performance testing**, and how to integrate automated testing into a **CI/CD pipeline**. We'll cover:

- **Unit Testing with JUnit and Mockito** for testing individual units of code

- **UI Testing with Espresso and UIAutomator** to automate UI interactions

- **Performance Testing with Firebase Test Lab** to assess app performance

- **CI/CD Pipelines with GitHub Actions and Firebase** for automated deployment and testing

- **Pro Tip: Automate UI testing for Play Store approval** to pass the app's submission process

By the end of this chapter, you will be equipped with the tools and techniques needed to set up a **comprehensive automated testing pipeline** for your Android app.

1. Unit Testing with JUnit & Mockito

1.1 What is Unit Testing?

Unit testing focuses on testing the **smallest pieces of code** (such as functions or methods) in isolation to ensure that they work as expected. It is essential for catching **logical errors** early and ensuring that the core functionality of your app remains intact as you add new features.

1.2 Why Use JUnit for Unit Testing?

JUnit is the **most widely used testing framework** for Java-based applications, including Android. It provides:

✓ **Annotations** (like @Test, @Before, @After) to define test methods and setup code

✓ **Assertions** (like assertEquals, assertTrue, assertNotNull) to check the expected outcomes of tests

✓ **Test suites** to organize and run multiple tests

Example JUnit Test Case:

kotlin

```kotlin
import org.junit.Test

import org.junit.Assert.*


class CalculatorTest {

    @Test

    fun testAddition() {

        val result = 2 + 2

        assertEquals(4, result)

    }

}
```

✓ The @Test annotation marks the method as a test, and assertEquals checks if the expected result matches the actual result.

1.3 Using Mockito for Mocking Dependencies

In unit tests, you often need to isolate the code from external dependencies, like database calls or network requests. **Mockito** allows you to **mock** these dependencies to ensure that tests focus only on the code being tested.

Step 1: Add Mockito Dependencies

gradle

```
dependencies {

    testImplementation 'org.mockito:mockito-core:4.0.0'

    testImplementation 'org.junit.jupiter:junit-jupiter-api:5.7.0'

}
```

Step 2: Create a Unit Test with Mocks

kotlin

```
class UserRepositoryTest {


    private val apiService: ApiService = mock(ApiService::class.java)

    private val userRepository = UserRepository(apiService)
```

```kotlin
@Test

fun testGetUserData() {

    val expectedUser = User("John", "john@example.com")

    `when`(apiService.getUser()).thenReturn(expectedUser)


    val result = userRepository.getUserData()


    assertEquals(expectedUser, result)

  }

}
```

✓ The mock function creates a mock of ApiService, and when is used to define what the mock should return when getUser() is called.

✓ **Mockito** allows you to isolate and test code without actual network calls, making tests faster and more reliable.

2. UI Testing with Espresso & UIAutomator

2.1 What is UI Testing?

UI testing ensures that the **user interface behaves as expected** when users interact with it. This includes checking whether buttons are clickable, whether text fields accept input, and whether navigation flows are working.

2.2 Why Use Espresso for UI Testing?

Espresso is a **popular UI testing framework** for Android. It enables you to simulate user actions and verify that the UI components respond correctly.

Example Espresso Test Case:

kotlin

```
import androidx.test.espresso.Espresso.*

import androidx.test.espresso.action.ViewActions.*

import androidx.test.espresso.matcher.ViewMatchers.*

import org.junit.Test
```

```
class LoginActivityTest {


    @Test

    fun testLogin() {


onView(withId(R.id.usernameField)).perform(typeText("user
123"), closeSoftKeyboard())


onView(withId(R.id.passwordField)).perform(typeText("pass
word"), closeSoftKeyboard())

        onView(withId(R.id.loginButton)).perform(click())


        onView(withText("Welcome,
user123")).check(matches(isDisplayed()))

    }

}
```

✓ **onView(withId())** locates UI elements by their IDs.

✓ **perform(typeText())** simulates typing text into a field.

✓ **perform(click())** simulates a button click.

✓ **check(matches())** verifies that the expected result occurs (e.g., a welcome message is displayed).

2.3 Using UIAutomator for Cross-App UI Testing

While Espresso is excellent for testing your app's UI, **UIAutomator** can interact with **system-level UI elements** (like the status bar or settings) and cross-app UI components.

Example UIAutomator Test Case:

kotlin

```
import androidx.test.uiautomator.*

import org.junit.Test


class SettingsTest {


    @Test

    fun testChangeLanguage() {
```

```kotlin
val device =
UiDevice.getInstance(InstrumentationRegistry.getInstrument
ation())


    device.pressHome()

    device.findObject(By.desc("Settings")).click()

    device.findObject(By.text("Language")).click()

    device.findObject(By.text("English")).click()


    assertTrue(device.findObject(By.text("Language
changed")).exists())

    }

}
```

✓ UIAutomator allows you to simulate user interactions with **system apps** and **settings**.
✓ It is useful for **end-to-end tests** involving multiple apps.

3. Performance Testing with Firebase Test Lab

3.1 What is Firebase Test Lab?

Firebase Test Lab is a **cloud-based testing service** that allows you to run **automated tests** on a wide range of **real Android devices** hosted by Google. It helps identify performance issues on different devices without needing physical access to them.

3.2 Benefits of Firebase Test Lab

✓ **Automated testing** across a wide range of Android devices

✓ **Simulates real-world scenarios**, such as network latency and battery usage

✓ Supports **Espresso, UIAutomator**, and **Game Loop** for gaming apps

3.3 Running Tests on Firebase Test Lab

Step 1: Configure Firebase Test Lab

You need to link your Android project with Firebase and set up the necessary dependencies in your **build.gradle** file.

Step 2: Run Tests Using the Firebase Console

1. Go to the **Firebase Console** and select **Test Lab**.

2. Select the **app** you want to test.

3. Choose from a list of **physical devices** and run your tests.

You can also automate the process via **CI/CD tools** like **GitHub Actions**.

4. CI/CD Pipelines with GitHub Actions & Firebase

4.1 What is CI/CD?

Continuous Integration (CI) and Continuous Deployment (CD) are practices that automate the process of **building, testing, and deploying** your app. This ensures that new changes are integrated smoothly without disrupting the app's stability.

4.2 Setting Up GitHub Actions for CI/CD

GitHub Actions provides a way to automate workflows for building and testing your Android app.

Step 1: Set Up GitHub Actions Workflow

Create a .github/workflows/android.yml file in your project to define the workflow:

yaml

```yaml
name: Android CI/CD Workflow

on:
  push:
    branches:
      - main
  pull_request:
    branches:
      - main

jobs:
  build:
    runs-on: ubuntu-latest
```

```
steps:

  - name: Checkout code

    uses: actions/checkout@v2

  - name: Set up JDK 11

    uses: actions/setup-java@v2

    with:

      java-version: 11

  - name: Build Release APK

    run: ./gradlew build

  - name: Run tests

    run: ./gradlew test
```

4.3 Integrating Firebase Test Lab with GitHub Actions

You can automate tests with **Firebase Test Lab** using GitHub Actions by invoking the Firebase Test Lab API. This step ensures that tests run in **real environments** after every commit.

Step 1: Set Up Firebase Test Lab API Key

Generate an **API key** from the Firebase Console and store it securely.

Step 2: Add Firebase Test Lab Step in GitHub Actions Workflow

yaml

```
- name: Run Firebase Test Lab

  run: |

    gcloud firebase test android run --type instrumentation --app
./app/build/outputs/apk/release/app-release.apk          --test
./app/build/outputs/androidTest-apk/debug/app-debug-
androidTest.apk --device model=Pixel4,version=28
```

Pro Tip: Automate UI Testing for Play Store Approval

Google requires that Android apps go through **automated UI tests** before being approved for the Play Store. **Automating UI testing** for **Play Store approval** is a key step in ensuring your app passes these tests without delays.

1. **Use Espresso tests** to simulate user interactions (e.g., logging in, navigating through menus).

2. **Ensure your app has no crashes or ANR issues** during the automated tests.

3. **Submit your automated test results** when you submit the app for review.

By incorporating **automated testing** into your CI/CD pipeline, you can ensure that your app is **Play Store-ready** and that future updates pass without issue.

SECTION 5: MONETIZATION, LOCALIZATION & AI FEATURES

Chapter 10: Monetization: Generating Revenue from Apps

Building a great Android app is only half the battle. To ensure the app remains sustainable and profitable, developers must integrate effective **monetization strategies**. Monetization not only provides revenue to support development but also helps you **keep your app free** for users while offering them additional value.

In this chapter, we will cover a variety of monetization strategies for Android apps, including:

- **In-App Purchases (IAP) & Google Play Billing**

- **Implementing AdMob & Rewarded Ads**

- **Subscription Models & Recurring Payments**

- **Case Study: How Top Apps Use Hybrid Monetization**

By the end of this chapter, you will be familiar with several **monetization methods** and how to integrate them seamlessly into your Android app, maximizing **revenue opportunities** while maintaining a great user experience.

1. In-App Purchases (IAP) & Google Play Billing

1.1 What Are In-App Purchases (IAP)?

In-app purchases allow you to sell digital goods or content **directly within your app**. Users can buy extra features, virtual goods, or unlock premium content without leaving the app. In-app purchases are popular in **freemium apps** (apps that are free to download but offer in-app purchases for additional features).

Types of In-App Purchases:

1. **Consumable Products**: These items can be **used up** and bought again (e.g., virtual coins in a game).

2. **Non-Consumable Products**: These items are purchased once and **unlocked permanently** (e.g., removing ads, premium features).

3. **Subscriptions**: These provide **access to content or services** for a specific period (e.g., monthly access to premium content).

1.2 Setting Up Google Play Billing

Google Play Billing allows developers to implement in-app purchases using the official **Google Play Billing Library**.

Step 1: Add Google Play Billing Dependency

gradle

```
dependencies {

    implementation 'com.android.billingclient:billing:5.0.0'

}
```

Step 2: Set Up Google Play Console

- Create your product listings in the **Google Play Console** (e.g., consumables, non-consumables, or subscriptions).

- Define **pricing, billing cycles**, and product IDs.

Step 3: Implementing IAP in Your App

1. **Create BillingClient**:

kotlin

```kotlin
val billingClient = BillingClient.newBuilder(context)

    .setListener { responseCode, purchases ->

        // Handle the purchase

    }

    .enablePendingPurchases() // Required for purchases to be
successful

    .build()
```

2. **Query Available Products**:

kotlin

```kotlin
val productList = listOf(

    QueryProductDetailsParams.Product.newBuilder()

        .setProductId("premium_upgrade")

        .setProductType(BillingClient.ProductType.INAPP)

        .build()

)
```

```kotlin
val params =
QueryProductDetailsParams.newBuilder().setProductList(productList).build()

billingClient.queryProductDetailsAsync(params) { billingResult, productDetailsList ->

    // Handle product details

}
```

3. **Handle Purchase Flow**:

kotlin

```kotlin
val flowParams = BillingFlowParams.newBuilder()
    .setSkuDetails(skuDetails)
    .build()
val responseCode = billingClient.launchBillingFlow(activity, flowParams)
```

1.3 Best Practices for IAP

✓ **Ensure a seamless purchase flow** – Avoid unnecessary steps that may confuse or frustrate users.

✓ **Offer value** – Make sure the in-app purchase enhances the user experience and justifies the cost.

✓ **Test thoroughly** – Use the **Google Play Console**'s internal testing tracks to validate purchases and ensure smooth functionality.

2. Implementing AdMob & Rewarded Ads

2.1 Why Use Ads for Monetization?

Ads are one of the most common ways to monetize free apps. They allow you to **earn revenue** without requiring users to make purchases. There are two types of ads typically used for monetization:

1. **Interstitial Ads** – Full-screen ads that appear at natural transition points, such as between game levels.

2. **Rewarded Ads** – Ads that offer **rewards** (such as in-game currency) in exchange for viewing an ad.

2.2 Setting Up AdMob in Your App

Step 1: Add AdMob SDK Dependencies

gradle

```
dependencies {

    implementation     'com.google.android.gms:play-services-
ads:22.1.0'

}
```

Step 2: Initialize AdMob in MainActivity

kotlin

```kotlin
MobileAds.initialize(this) { }
```

Step 3: Create and Load an Ad

For **Rewarded Ads**:

kotlin

```kotlin
val rewardedAd = RewardedAd(this, "your_ad_unit_id")

rewardedAd.loadAd(AdRequest.Builder().build(),   object   :
RewardedAdLoadCallback() {
```

```kotlin
override fun onAdLoaded() {

    // The ad has loaded successfully

}


override fun onAdFailedToLoad(errorCode: Int) {

    // Handle the failure

}
})
```

Step 4: Show the Ad

kotlin

```kotlin
if (rewardedAd.isLoaded) {

  rewardedAd.show(this) { rewardItem ->

    // Grant the reward to the user

  }

}
```

Step 5: Handle User Interactions

Ensure that users are **properly rewarded** only after watching the full ad. If they skip the ad, they should **not receive the reward**.

2.3 Best Practices for Implementing Ads

✓ **Do not overwhelm users with ads** – Make sure ads are shown at **logical points** (such as between levels in a game).

✓ **Use rewarded ads strategically** – Offer rewards for actions that enhance the user experience (e.g., extra lives, in-game currency).

✓ **Test ad performance** – Use **AdMob mediation** to optimize revenue by serving the best-performing ad networks.

3. Subscription Models & Recurring Payments

3.1 Why Use Subscription Models?

Subscriptions provide a **steady, recurring revenue stream** and are ideal for apps that offer **premium content or services**.

Popular subscription-based apps include **streaming platforms, fitness apps**, and **news apps**.

Subscriptions can be classified into two types:

1. **Auto-Renewing Subscriptions** – These are automatically renewed (e.g., monthly, yearly).

2. **Non-Renewing Subscriptions** – These require the user to manually renew the subscription after a period.

3.2 Setting Up Subscriptions with Google Play Billing

Step 1: Create Subscription in Google Play Console

- Go to the **Google Play Console** and set up a **new subscription** product with a price and billing period (e.g., monthly or yearly).

Step 2: Implement Subscription Flow in App

Follow the same basic process as IAP but for **subscription products**. Use BillingClient to query available subscriptions and launch the billing flow:

kotlin

```kotlin
val subscriptionProduct =
QueryProductDetailsParams.Product.newBuilder()

    .setProductId("premium_subscription")

    .setProductType(BillingClient.ProductType.SUBS)

    .build()

val params =
QueryProductDetailsParams.newBuilder().setProductList(list
Of(subscriptionProduct)).build()

billingClient.queryProductDetailsAsync(params) {
billingResult, productDetailsList ->

    // Handle the subscription response

}
```

Step 3: Handle Subscription Activation

kotlin

```kotlin
val flowParams = BillingFlowParams.newBuilder()

    .setSkuDetails(subscriptionSkuDetails)

    .build()
```

```kotlin
val responseCode = billingClient.launchBillingFlow(activity,
flowParams)
```

3.3 Best Practices for Subscription Models

✓ **Offer free trials** – Allow users to try out the subscription content or features before committing to a paid plan.

✓ **Clearly communicate the value** – Make sure users understand what they get with the subscription.

✓ **Send reminders before renewal** – Notify users in advance of upcoming payments to **minimize churn**.

✓ **Easy cancellation process** – Make it simple for users to cancel subscriptions directly within the app.

4. Case Study: How Top Apps Use Hybrid Monetization

4.1 Hybrid Monetization Strategy Overview

Hybrid monetization involves combining multiple revenue streams, such as **in-app purchases, ads, and subscriptions**, to maximize app earnings. Top apps like **Spotify**, **TikTok**, and **YouTube** use a **hybrid approach** to cater to different user preferences.

4.2 Case Study: TikTok's Hybrid Monetization

TikTok utilizes both **ads and in-app purchases** for monetization, enabling the platform to appeal to a wide range of users. TikTok's revenue model includes:

1. **In-App Purchases**: Users can buy **virtual coins** to give gifts to content creators during live streams.

2. **Ad Revenue**: TikTok generates revenue through **display ads** that appear during users' feeds, as well as **branded effects** and **video ads**.

3. **Subscriptions**: TikTok also offers **premium features** for creators, such as analytics and additional tools for managing their accounts.

How TikTok Maximizes Revenue:

✓ **In-app purchases** for virtual goods keep users engaged while offering **exclusive interactions**.

✓ **Ads** are displayed in a non-intrusive way, appearing naturally as users scroll through their feed.

✓ **Subscriptions** are aimed at power users who seek **enhanced tools** to improve their content creation.

4.3 Case Study: Spotify's Hybrid Monetization

Spotify also uses a hybrid monetization approach, including:

1. **Subscriptions**: Premium subscribers get **ad-free listening, offline playlists**, and **high-quality audio**.

2. **Ads**: Free users listen to **ads between songs** but still enjoy the core features of the platform.

3. **In-App Purchases**: Spotify occasionally offers **add-ons** like **Spotify Wrapped** for additional personalized features.

Chapter 11: Internationalization & Localization for Global Markets

The global app market continues to grow, and as an Android developer, expanding your app to **multiple languages and regions** can significantly increase its reach and user base. **Internationalization (i18n)** and **localization (l10n)** are essential for ensuring your app provides a seamless experience for users around the world.

- **Internationalization (i18n)** is the process of designing your app so that it can support **multiple languages** and **regional settings** without requiring significant changes to the code.

- **Localization (l10n)** involves adapting the app to specific languages, cultures, and regions, ensuring that the app feels native to the users in those areas.

In this chapter, we will explore:

- **Adapting UI and text for different languages**

- **Handling currency, date formats, and regional differences**

- **Using Firebase Remote Config for real-time localization updates**

- **Checklist: Preparing your app for international markets**

By the end of this chapter, you will be equipped to make your app **global-ready**, providing users with a native-like experience no matter where they are located.

1. Adapting UI & Text for Different Languages

1.1 Why Localization Matters

When expanding your app to global markets, it's crucial to **adapt your user interface (UI)** to support **different languages** and **cultural norms**. Without localization, your app may appear unprofessional or difficult to use in regions where the language or culture differs from your original market.

Key Points for Localization:

- **Text Translation** – Translate static and dynamic text elements to different languages.

- **UI Adjustments** – Ensure that the layout and design can accommodate varying text lengths, reading directions, and cultural preferences.

1.2 Adapting Text for Different Languages

Android supports localization by using **resource files** to manage different languages. These files are stored in the res/values directory and follow the **language and country codes**.

Step 1: Create Language-Specific Resource Files

You can define language-specific strings in **strings.xml** files. For example, for English (default) and Spanish, you would create:

- res/values/strings.xml (for English)

- res/values-es/strings.xml (for Spanish)

Example for English (res/values/strings.xml):

xml

```
<resources>

    <string name="app_name">My Android App</string>

    <string name="greeting">Hello, welcome to the app!</string>

</resources>
```

Example for Spanish (res/values-es/strings.xml):

xml

```
<resources>

    <string name="app_name">Mi aplicación Android</string>

    <string name="greeting">¡Hola, bienvenido a la
aplicación!</string>

</resources>
```

When the app runs on a **Spanish device**, Android will automatically load the Spanish version of the strings from values-es/strings.xml. This allows you to provide **localized text** without changing the app's core functionality.

1.3 Handling UI Layouts for Different Languages

Different languages have different **text lengths** and **reading directions**, which can affect the layout. For instance, **German** text can often be longer than English text, while **Arabic** is read from right to left.

1.3.1 Text Direction (LTR vs. RTL)

To accommodate languages like **Arabic** or **Hebrew**, which are read from **right to left (RTL)**, Android supports **RTL layouts**.

This is done automatically if the system language is set to an RTL language, but you can also set the layoutDirection programmatically.

Example: Handling RTL Layouts

kotlin

```
val layoutDirection = if (isRtlLanguage) {

    View.LAYOUT_DIRECTION_RTL

} else {

    View.LAYOUT_DIRECTION_LTR

}

view.layoutDirection = layoutDirection
```

1.3.2 Adjusting UI Components for Different Text Lengths

When designing layouts, ensure that **UI components are flexible** and can handle varying text lengths. Use **wrap_content** for text elements and **match_parent** for buttons or other components to ensure they adapt to the content.

For example, instead of setting a fixed size for a button:

xml

```
<Button

    android:layout_width="wrap_content"

    android:layout_height="wrap_content"

    android:text="@string/submit"/>
```

This allows the button to **expand or contract** based on the language and text length.

2. Handling Currency, Date Formats, & Regional Differences

2.1 Adapting to Regional Currency Formats

Different regions have **different currency symbols, decimal separators**, and **grouping separators**. For example, in the United States, the currency format is $1,000.00, while in Germany, it's 1.000,00 €. Android provides utilities to handle this automatically through the NumberFormat class.

Example: Formatting Currency Based on Locale

kotlin

```
val currency = Currency.getInstance("EUR")
val                    numberFormat                    =
NumberFormat.getCurrencyInstance(Locale("de", "DE"))
val formattedCurrency = numberFormat.format(1000.0)
Log.d("Currency", formattedCurrency)  // Output: 1.000,00 €
```

This allows the app to **automatically format currency** based on the device's locale, ensuring that users see the correct symbols and decimal separators for their region.

2.2 Handling Date Formats

Date formats differ from region to region. For example, in the **US**, the format is MM/DD/YYYY, while in **Europe**, it's DD/MM/YYYY. Use DateFormat and SimpleDateFormat to adapt to these differences.

Example: Formatting Dates Based on Locale

```kotlin
val                    dateFormat                    =
DateFormat.getDateInstance(DateFormat.LONG, Locale("fr",
"FR"))

val date = Date()

val formattedDate = dateFormat.format(date)

Log.d("Date", formattedDate)  // Output: 10 juillet 2023
```

This ensures that your app **displays the date correctly** for each user's region.

2.3 Handling Time Zones

When dealing with **time-sensitive operations**, you must consider **time zone differences**. Android provides a TimeZone class to handle this.

Example: Converting Time Based on Time Zone

```kotlin
```

```kotlin
val timeZone = TimeZone.getTimeZone("America/New_York")

val calendar = Calendar.getInstance(timeZone)

val time = calendar.time

val formattedTime = SimpleDateFormat("HH:mm:ss", Locale.getDefault()).format(time)

Log.d("Time", formattedTime)  // Output: Time based on New York timezone
```

3. Using Firebase Remote Config for Real-Time Localization Updates

3.1 What is Firebase Remote Config?

Firebase Remote Config allows you to **remotely update the app's settings and content** without requiring an app update. This can be useful for **real-time localization**, as you can change text, UI layouts, and settings dynamically based on the user's region.

3.2 Setting Up Firebase Remote Config

Step 1: Add Firebase Dependencies

gradle

```
dependencies {

  implementation        'com.google.firebase:firebase-config-
ktx:21.0.1'

}
```

Step 2: Initialize Firebase Remote Config

kotlin

```
val firebaseConfig = FirebaseRemoteConfig.getInstance()

firebaseConfig.setConfigSettingsAsync(

  RemoteConfigSettings.Builder()

    .setMinimumFetchIntervalInSeconds(3600)

    .build()

)
```

Step 3: Fetch and Apply Remote Config Parameters

kotlin

```kotlin
firebaseConfig.fetchAndActivate()
    .addOnCompleteListener { task ->
        if (task.isSuccessful) {
            val configValue =
firebaseConfig.getString("welcome_message")
            textView.text = configValue  // Dynamically update UI text
        }
    }
```

3.3 Use Cases for Firebase Remote Config in Localization

- **Dynamic language changes**: If you support multiple languages, you can **change text dynamically** based on the user's locale.

- **Feature toggles**: Enable or disable certain features based on the region or market.

- **Content updates**: Change content (e.g., advertisements or offers) based on the user's region without requiring an app update.

4. Checklist: Preparing Your App for International Markets

4.1 Internationalization Checklist

- ⌐ **Ensure Unicode Support** – Use UTF-8 encoding to support special characters from various languages.

- ⌐ **Plan for RTL Layouts** – If supporting languages like Arabic or Hebrew, ensure the app handles **right-to-left (RTL) text** properly.

- ⌐ **Design Flexible Layouts** – Make sure your UI components **scale** based on text size and language, including buttons and form fields.

- ⌐ **Use Plurals** – For languages that have plural forms (e.g., English: "1 item", "2 items"), use **plurals** in strings.xml.

- ⌐ **Provide Locale-Specific Assets** – Different regions may require **different images, icons, or formats**. Use resource directories such as res/drawable-en, res/drawable-fr, etc.

- ⌐ **Support Local Time and Date Formats** – Use the appropriate locale-specific formats for **dates**, **times**, and **currencies**.

- ⌐ **Offer Multiple Payment Methods** – Different regions may have **different preferred payment methods** (e.g., PayPal, Google Pay, credit cards).

4.2 Localization Checklist

- ⌐ **Translate All UI Text** – Ensure that all UI elements (buttons, labels, titles) are **translated into target languages**.

- ⌐ **Test Layouts in Multiple Languages** – Ensure that **text expansion** (e.g., in German) or **contraction** (e.g., in Chinese) doesn't break your UI.

- **Support Regional Variations** – Account for **regional dialects, currencies**, and **cultural differences** in your localization process.

- **Test on Real Devices** – Always test localized versions of the app on **real devices** to catch layout issues or crashes.

- **Implement Remote Localization** – Use **Firebase Remote Config** to easily update content and text in your app without needing an app update.

Chapter 12: AI & Machine Learning in Android Apps

Artificial Intelligence (AI) and Machine Learning (ML) are transforming industries, and **Android apps** are no exception. With advancements in AI, developers now have the tools to create apps that can **understand user behavior, make intelligent recommendations, recognize images**, and even **engage in conversations**. These capabilities elevate the user experience and provide highly personalized interactions.

In this chapter, we will explore how to integrate **AI and ML** into your Android apps, focusing on:

- **Integrating TensorFlow Lite** for **on-device AI** processing

- **Implementing AI-powered recommendations**, such as content suggestions

- **Creating AI chatbots and voice assistants** using the **Google Assistant API**

- **Using AI-based image recognition** and **OCR (Optical Character Recognition)** for text extraction

- **Mini-Challenge**: Building an AI-powered search feature

By the end of this chapter, you will have the knowledge to **incorporate cutting-edge AI technologies** into your Android apps, making them more intelligent, responsive, and engaging.

1. Integrating TensorFlow Lite for On-Device AI

1.1 What is TensorFlow Lite?

TensorFlow Lite (TFLite) is a lightweight, optimized version of **TensorFlow** designed specifically for mobile and embedded devices. It allows you to deploy machine learning models directly onto Android devices, ensuring **faster inference** and **offline capability**. TFLite supports both **vision and speech models**, making it perfect for apps that require real-time predictions like image classification, object detection, or language translation.

1.2 Why Use TensorFlow Lite?

- **Performance**: TFLite is optimized for mobile hardware, including **CPU**, **GPU**, and **DSP**.

- **Small size**: It ensures that machine learning models are **lightweight**, saving device storage.

- **Offline operation**: AI models can run entirely on the device, without relying on server-side computation, ensuring faster predictions and **privacy** for sensitive data.

1.3 Adding TensorFlow Lite to Your Android Project

To get started with TensorFlow Lite, follow these steps:

Step 1: Add Dependencies In your **build.gradle** file, add the following dependencies to integrate TensorFlow Lite into your Android app:

gradle

```
dependencies {

    implementation 'org.tensorflow:tensorflow-lite:2.7.0'

    implementation 'org.tensorflow:tensorflow-lite-gpu:2.7.0' // For GPU acceleration (optional)

    implementation                'org.tensorflow:tensorflow-lite-support:2.7.0'

}
```

Step 2: Prepare Your Model You can use pre-trained models available from TensorFlow or train your own model. Once trained, convert your model to the TensorFlow Lite format (.tflite) using TensorFlow's conversion tool. You can also optimize models for mobile devices using **post-training quantization** to reduce their size.

python

```python
import tensorflow as tf

model = tf.keras.models.load_model('path_to_model')

converter = tf.lite.TFLiteConverter.from_keras_model(model)

tflite_model = converter.convert()

with open('model.tflite', 'wb') as f:

    f.write(tflite_model)
```

Step 3: Load and Run the Model in Your App

To use the model in your app, load it with TensorFlow Lite's **Interpreter**:

kotlin

```kotlin
val   tfliteModel   =   FileUtil.loadMappedFile(context,
"model.tflite")
```

```kotlin
val tfliteInterpreter = Interpreter(tfliteModel)
```

Step 4: Make Predictions with the Model

kotlin

```kotlin
val input = arrayOf(1.0f, 2.0f)  // Input data (example)
val output = Array(1) { FloatArray(1) }  // Output array

tfliteInterpreter.run(input, output)
Log.d("Prediction", "Output: ${output[0][0]}")
```

This code uses TensorFlow Lite to run the model on the device and get a prediction. It's designed to be **fast, efficient**, and **run entirely offline**.

2. Implementing AI-Powered Recommendations

2.1 What Are AI-Powered Recommendations?

AI-powered recommendations use **machine learning models** to predict and suggest content, products, or services that users are likely to engage with. Common examples include:

- **Content suggestions** in video streaming apps like YouTube or Netflix

- **Product recommendations** in e-commerce apps like Amazon or eBay

- **Song recommendations** in music apps like Spotify

These systems rely on **collaborative filtering** and **content-based filtering**, where the app learns from users' behavior and preferences.

2.2 Building AI-Powered Recommendation System

To build an AI-powered recommendation system, follow these basic steps:

Step 1: Collect Data You need to collect user data on their preferences, interactions, and activities within the app. This data can include:

- User ratings

- Items watched, liked, or purchased

- User demographics (e.g., age, location)

Step 2: Train a Recommendation Model Using a machine learning algorithm like **Matrix Factorization, k-nearest neighbors (k-NN)**, or **Neural Networks**, you can build a recommendation model. For example, using TensorFlow, you can create a collaborative filtering model.

Step 3: Integrate the Model with Your App

Once the recommendation model is trained, convert it to TensorFlow Lite format and integrate it into your Android app as described earlier. After that, you can use the model to make personalized recommendations for each user.

kotlin

```
// Example pseudo-code for recommendation logic

val                    recommendedItems             =
recommendationModel.getRecommendations(userId)

displayRecommendations(recommendedItems)
```

3. Creating AI Chatbots & Voice Assistants Using Google Assistant API

3.1 What is the Google Assistant API?

The **Google Assistant API** allows you to integrate **voice interactions** with your Android app. By connecting your app to the **Google Assistant**, you can provide users with a **natural language interface** to interact with your app. For example, users could say, "**Play music**," and the assistant will respond by playing their favorite playlist.

3.2 How to Implement AI Chatbots and Voice Assistants

Step 1: Set Up the Google Assistant SDK

You can use the **Actions on Google** SDK to integrate Google Assistant into your app. First, you must **create an action** in the **Actions on Google Console**.

Step 2: Build the Action and Fulfillment Endpoint

Define the **intents** (commands like "play music" or "show the weather") in the **Dialogflow console**, and then create a backend service (using **Firebase Functions** or **Google Cloud**), which will handle the requests.

javascript

```javascript
const { dialogflow } = require('actions-on-google');

const app = dialogflow();


app.intent('Default Welcome Intent', (conv) => {

  conv.ask('Hi! How can I help you today?');

});
```

Step 3: Deploy and Test Your Assistant

Once the action is developed and deployed, you can integrate it with your Android app using **Google Assistant SDK** and let users interact with the app using voice commands.

kotlin

```kotlin
val assistant = Assistant.getInstance(context)

assistant.query("Play my favorite playlist")
```

4. Using AI-Based Image Recognition & OCR (Text Extraction)

4.1 What is Image Recognition?

Image recognition is the process of identifying objects or features within images. In Android, you can use machine learning models to recognize faces, objects, text, and more.

4.2 Integrating Image Recognition with TensorFlow Lite

You can implement **image classification models** using TensorFlow Lite. For example, you could use **object detection** models (like **MobileNet** or **YOLO**) to identify items in photos or images.

Example: Running an Image Classification Model

kotlin

```kotlin
val imageBitmap = BitmapFactory.decodeFile(imagePath)

val tensorImage = TensorImage.fromBitmap(imageBitmap)

val outputMap = HashMap<Int, TensorBuffer>()

tfliteInterpreter.run(tensorImage.buffer, outputMap)
```

```
val result = outputMap[0]?.floatArray
```

This code loads an image and uses a pre-trained model to identify objects in the image.

4.3 Optical Character Recognition (OCR)

OCR allows apps to **extract text** from images. Using the **ML Kit** library, you can easily integrate OCR into your Android app to scan documents, images, and other text-heavy media.

Step 1: Add Dependencies

gradle

```
dependencies {
    implementation 'com.google.mlkit:text-recognition:16.0.0'
}
```

Step 2: Implement OCR in Your App

kotlin

```kotlin
val recognizer =
TextRecognition.getClient(TextRecognizerOptions.DEFAUL
T_OPTIONS)

val inputImage = InputImage.fromBitmap(bitmap, 0)


recognizer.process(inputImage)

    .addOnSuccessListener { visionText ->

        val recognizedText = visionText.text

        // Use recognized text

    }

    .addOnFailureListener { e ->

        Log.e("OCR", "Text recognition failed", e)

    }
```

This will extract the text from an image and allow your app to **process the information** (e.g., extract address details from an ID card).

5. Mini-Challenge: Build an AI-Powered Search Feature

Challenge Objective:

Build a **search feature** in your app that uses **AI-powered recommendations** to suggest content based on user preferences. The app should use a combination of **TensorFlow Lite**, **Firebase Remote Config**, and **content filtering models** to suggest relevant content.

Challenge Steps:

1. **Train a recommendation model** based on user activity (e.g., viewed items, ratings).

2. **Integrate the model into the app** using TensorFlow Lite.

3. **Build a search interface** that filters results using the recommendation model.

4. **Implement Firebase Remote Config** to fetch personalized settings for users in real-time.

5. **Add an AI-powered recommendation button** to enhance search results with content that matches user interests.

SECTION 6: PUBLISHING, MAINTENANCE & FUTURE TRENDS

Chapter 13: Preparing & Publishing an App on Google Play

The journey from **app development** to **launch** is one of the most exciting phases of app creation. But before your app reaches users, it's crucial to **prepare** it for submission and ensure it's optimized for the **Google Play Store**. This chapter will guide you through the essential steps of **preparing, optimizing**, and **publishing** your Android app on the Google Play Store, so it reaches its full potential in terms of **visibility, usability**, and **downloads**.

We will cover:

- **Generating signed APKs and AABs** to prepare your app for release

- **Play Store Optimization (ASO)** techniques for driving more downloads

- **Beta Testing** and managing user feedback to ensure your app's quality

- **Checklist: Essential steps before app submission** to ensure a smooth and successful launch

By the end of this chapter, you will have a solid understanding of the **publishing process** and be prepared to submit your app to the **Google Play Store** with confidence.

1. Generating Signed APKs & AABs

1.1 What is an APK?

An **APK (Android Package Kit)** is the file format used to distribute and install applications on Android devices. It's essentially the app's **installation file**, containing everything needed to run the app, including **code, resources**, and **assets**.

1.2 What is an AAB?

An **AAB (Android App Bundle)** is a newer, more efficient format for delivering Android apps. Unlike APKs, AABs are **not directly installed on devices**. Instead, they are **uploaded to the Google Play Console**, where Google Play automatically generates and serves optimized APKs for different devices, reducing app size and improving delivery efficiency.

AABs provide several advantages:

- **Reduced APK size**: By packaging the app as a bundle, it can be split into multiple APKs tailored for different devices (e.g., different screen sizes or CPU architectures).

- **Better app delivery**: Google Play dynamically serves the right APK, reducing download sizes for users.

- **Required for new apps**: Starting in **August 2021**, Google Play now **requires new apps** to be submitted as **AABs** rather than APKs.

1.3 Generating a Signed APK or AAB

Before submitting your app to the Play Store, you need to **sign** it with a **secure key** to ensure its authenticity. Here's how to generate a signed APK or AAB:

Step 1: Create a Keystore File

To sign your APK or AAB, you need a **keystore file** containing the **private key**. You can create one using **Android Studio**:

1. Go to **Build > Generate Signed Bundle / APK**.

2. Select **Android App Bundle** or **APK**.

3. Choose **Create new...** for the keystore.

4. Enter the required details like the keystore password, key alias, and validity period.

Step 2: Sign the APK or AAB

Once the keystore is created, sign the APK or AAB:

1. In **Android Studio**, go to **Build** > **Generate Signed Bundle / APK**.

2. Choose **APK** or **Android App Bundle** and click **Next**.

3. Select the **keystore** you created and enter the password and alias.

4. Select **Release** build type, and click **Finish**.

Android Studio will generate a signed APK or AAB ready for submission to the Play Store.

2. Play Store Optimization (ASO) for More Downloads

2.1 What is ASO (App Store Optimization)?

ASO (App Store Optimization) is the process of optimizing an app's **visibility** in the Play Store, making it easier for users to discover and download the app. Effective ASO can lead to **increased downloads** and **better rankings** in search results.

Key ASO factors include:

- **App Title** and **Description**

- **App Icon** and **Screenshots**

- **Keywords** and **Reviews**

2.2 Key Elements of ASO

2.2.1 App Title & Description

The **app title** is one of the first things users see, so it's essential to make it **short, descriptive**, and **keyword-rich**. Including relevant **keywords** can improve your app's discoverability in search results.

- **App Title**: Choose a title that clearly explains what your app does and includes **relevant keywords**.

Example:

"MyFitness App: Track Workouts and Goals" is better than just "MyFitness App."

- **App Description**: Your description should be **clear and concise**, outlining the main features and benefits of your app. It should contain relevant **keywords** without overstuffing.

- **Short Description**: This is the snippet of text that appears under the app title on the Play Store. It should be compelling and summarize the app's core function in **a few words**.

2.2.2 App Icon & Screenshots

- **App Icon**: The icon is the first visual element users see when searching for apps. Make sure your icon is **unique**, **professional**, and **reflects your brand**.

- **Screenshots**: Include **high-quality screenshots** that showcase your app's **best features**. This is critical for potential users to understand the value your app provides.

2.2.3 Keywords and Localized Content

Google Play allows you to set **localized versions** of your app's content (including title, description, and keywords) for different regions and languages. Make sure to **optimize your app for different markets**.

- **Localization**: If you plan to target non-English-speaking regions, ensure you localize both the app description and visuals (screenshots, videos, etc.).

- **Keyword Research**: Use tools like **Google Keyword Planner** and **App Annie** to find the best keywords for your app. Choose keywords that have **high search volume** and **low competition**.

2.2.4 Ratings & Reviews

User feedback is one of the most important factors for ranking in the Play Store. **Good reviews** help build **trust** and **credibility**, while **low ratings** can hurt your app's visibility.

- **Encourage Positive Reviews**: Prompt users to leave a review after they have had a **positive experience** with your app. You can use tools like **In-App Review API** to streamline this process.

- **Respond to Reviews**: Engaging with users' feedback shows that you care about their experience and can help improve your ratings.

2.3 Tips for Effective ASO

- **Regular Updates**: Keep your app **updated** regularly to ensure it works with the latest versions of Android and to provide **new features**.

- **Analyze Metrics**: Use Google Play Console's **performance metrics** to track installs, ratings, and uninstalls.

- **A/B Testing**: Conduct A/B tests to optimize your **app title**, **icon**, and **description** to see which elements perform better.

3. Beta Testing & Managing User Feedback

3.1 Why Beta Testing is Important

Beta testing is crucial for understanding how your app performs in **real-world scenarios** and identifying bugs or issues before the official release. By gathering **feedback from users**, you can make necessary improvements and ensure your app functions as intended.

3.2 Setting Up Beta Testing

Google Play offers a **beta testing** feature that allows you to test your app with a limited number of users before launching it to the public. There are two types of beta testing:

1. **Closed Beta** – Invite only selected users to test your app.

2. **Open Beta** – Allow anyone to join the beta and try out your app.

Step 1: Create a Beta Testing Release in Google Play Console

1. Go to the **Google Play Console** and select your app.

2. Navigate to **Release Management** > **App Releases**.

3. Choose the **Beta track** and upload your APK/AAB.

Step   2:   Invite   Testers
For closed testing, you can upload a list of **email addresses** to invite users. For open testing, you can share a **public link** for users to join the beta.

3.3 Collecting User Feedback

User feedback is essential for improving your app. There are two main ways to collect feedback:

1. **In-App Feedback**: Add a feature within your app that allows users to send feedback directly to you.

Example:

kotlin

```kotlin
val intent = Intent(Intent.ACTION_SENDTO).apply {

    data = Uri.parse("mailto:youremail@example.com")

    putExtra(Intent.EXTRA_SUBJECT, "App Feedback")

}
startActivity(intent)
```

2. **Google Play Reviews**: Monitor **user reviews** on the Play Store and reply to them promptly to show that you care about feedback.

4. Checklist: Essential Steps Before App Submission

4.1 Pre-Submission Checklist

- ⌐ **Test thoroughly**: Ensure your app runs smoothly on **multiple devices** and Android versions.

- ⌐ **Optimize for performance**: Ensure that your app loads quickly, is responsive, and uses minimal system resources.

- ⌐ **Create a privacy policy**: If your app collects personal data, make sure you include a **clear privacy policy**.

- ⌐ **Prepare app assets**: Ensure your **app icon**, **screenshots**, and **video** are ready and high-quality.

- ⌐ **Localized content**: Ensure the app is **localized** for key markets (e.g., multiple languages, currencies, and time zones).

- ☐ **Check app size**: Verify that your app size is within **Play Store limits** (100MB for APKs, no limit for AABs).

- ☐ **Set up Google Play Console**: Make sure you have entered accurate **pricing, availability**, and **content rating**.

Chapter 14: Continuous Updates & App Maintenance

Launching an app on the **Google Play Store** is just the beginning of your app's lifecycle. After release, **continuous updates and maintenance** are critical to ensure your app remains **relevant**, **bug-free**, and **compatible** with new Android versions and device specifications. Regular updates help you stay ahead of bugs, improve user experience, and even expand your app's features, keeping your users engaged.

In this chapter, we'll explore strategies and tools for maintaining your app and rolling out **continuous updates**, including:

- **Handling app updates and versioning**

- **Using feature flags for controlled rollouts**

- **Crash reporting and analytics** (using tools like Firebase and Sentry)

- **Pro Tip: Handling negative reviews effectively**

By the end of this chapter, you will be prepared to manage your app after its release, ensuring it continues to deliver value to your users and grows over time.

1. Handling App Updates & Versioning

1.1 Why Regular Updates Matter

Regular app updates are essential for maintaining a **healthy app ecosystem**. These updates provide several benefits:

- **Bug fixes**: Address issues reported by users or found in testing.

- **Feature improvements**: Add new functionalities or enhance existing features.

- **Security patches**: Address vulnerabilities and ensure your app is safe.

- **Performance optimizations**: Improve app responsiveness and reduce resource usage.

Failure to update your app regularly can result in **negative user experiences**, **app crashes**, and **poor ratings**, leading to **declines in downloads** and even **uninstalls**.

1.2 Versioning Best Practices

App versioning helps developers and users understand the state of an app and track changes over time. Proper versioning is especially important when rolling out new features, fixing bugs, or ensuring compatibility with the latest Android OS versions.

Versioning Guidelines:

- **Semantic Versioning**: The general format of versioning is MAJOR.MINOR.PATCH.

  - **MAJOR**: Increment when you introduce **breaking changes** (i.e., changes that might break backward compatibility).

  - **MINOR**: Increment for **backward-compatible changes** that add functionality (e.g., new features or improvements).

  - **PATCH**: Increment for **bug fixes**, **security patches**, or **minor updates**.

Example:

- 1.0.0: Initial release.

- 1.1.0: New features added without breaking changes.

- 1.1.1: Bug fix for a crash.

1.3 Handling App Versioning in the Google Play Console

When you upload a new APK or AAB to Google Play, you must specify the **version code** and **version name** in your app's manifest file.

- **Version Code**: A unique integer used to identify the version of your app. This must be **incremented** with each release.

- **Version Name**: A string that represents the version visible to users (e.g., "1.2.0").

Example in build.gradle:

gradle

```
android {

  defaultConfig {

    versionCode 2
```

```
    versionName "1.1.0"

  }

}
```

When updating your app, ensure that the **version code** is incremented and the **version name** matches the new release.

1.4 Rollback Strategies for App Updates

Sometimes, even well-tested updates can introduce issues in the production environment. Having a rollback plan in place ensures you can quickly revert to a **stable version** of your app if necessary. Here are some strategies for rolling back:

- **Keep previous versions**: Always **keep the previous APK or AAB** version handy, so you can re-upload it in case of critical issues.

- **Implement A/B testing**: For critical updates or features, roll out the changes to a small percentage of users before expanding to the whole audience.

2. Using Feature Flags for Controlled Rollouts

2.1 What Are Feature Flags?

A **feature flag** (or **feature toggle**) is a powerful technique for **controlling the visibility of app features** in real-time. Instead of building separate app versions for testing, you can release new features to **specific groups of users** using flags that toggle functionality on or off.

Feature flags provide several benefits:

- **Controlled Rollouts**: Gradually roll out new features to specific users, minimizing the risk of introducing bugs.

- **A/B Testing**: Test new features with different user segments and gather data on their effectiveness before launching to the entire user base.

- **Instant Control**: Quickly enable or disable features without needing to update the app.

2.2 Implementing Feature Flags

To implement feature flags in your app, you can use a variety of tools. One popular choice is **Firebase Remote Config**, which allows you to remotely manage feature flags and other app settings.

Step 1: Add Firebase Remote Config Dependency

gradle

```
dependencies {

    implementation                 'com.google.firebase:firebase-
config:21.0.1'

}
```

Step 2: Fetch Remote Config Settings

kotlin

```
val firebaseConfig = FirebaseRemoteConfig.getInstance()

firebaseConfig.fetchAndActivate()

    .addOnCompleteListener { task ->

        if (task.isSuccessful) {
```

```
val                featureEnabled                =
firebaseConfig.getBoolean("new_feature_enabled")

    if (featureEnabled) {

        // Show the new feature

    }

  }

}
```

In this example, the app checks if the **new feature** is enabled remotely. Based on this flag, the app can **show or hide** the feature for the user.

2.3 Best Practices for Using Feature Flags

- **Start small**: Initially enable the feature for a **small percentage** of your users and gradually increase the user base.

- **Track metrics**: Monitor how the feature performs with the flagged users, measuring user engagement, crash rates, and other important metrics.

- **Clear expiration**: Feature flags should not be permanent; they should have an **expiration date** to ensure they're used only as intended.

3. Crash Reporting & Analytics (Firebase, Sentry)

3.1 Why Crash Reporting is Critical

Crash reporting is essential for identifying and fixing **bugs and crashes** that affect your app's stability. Even the most thoroughly tested apps can encounter errors in production, and it's vital to track and resolve them quickly.

Google Play Console offers basic crash reports, but **Firebase Crashlytics** and **Sentry** provide more comprehensive crash reporting and insights.

3.2 Using Firebase Crashlytics for Real-Time Crash Reporting

Firebase Crashlytics is a powerful crash reporting tool that helps developers monitor app stability and diagnose issues in real time.

Step 1: Add Firebase Crashlytics Dependency

gradle

```
dependencies {
    implementation 'com.google.firebase:firebase-crashlytics:18.2.6'
}
```

Step 2: Initialize Crashlytics in Your App

kotlin

```
FirebaseCrashlytics.getInstance().log("App launched")
FirebaseCrashlytics.getInstance().setUserId("user123")
```

Step 3: Log Custom Errors

You can log custom errors to track specific issues in your app, such as network failures or specific user actions.

kotlin

```kotlin
try {
    val data = fetchDataFromNetwork()
} catch (e: Exception) {
    FirebaseCrashlytics.getInstance().recordException(e)
}
```

Crashlytics automatically tracks **unhandled exceptions** and provides detailed reports on the **stack trace**, **device information**, and **steps leading to the crash**.

3.3 Using Sentry for Error Tracking

Sentry is another popular tool for tracking errors and performance issues in apps. It provides detailed reports on **exceptions, performance monitoring**, and **user sessions**.

Step 1: Add Sentry Dependency

gradle

```
dependencies {

    implementation 'io.sentry:sentry-android:4.3.0'

}
```

Step 2: Initialize Sentry in Your App

kotlin

```
Sentry.init { options ->

    options.dsn = "https://yourdsn@sentry.io/1234567"

}
```

Step 3: Track Errors

kotlin

```
try {

    // Simulate an error

    val result = 1 / 0

} catch (e: Exception) {

    Sentry.captureException(e)
```

}

3.4 Analytics for Tracking User Behavior

Alongside crash reporting, **analytics** tools like **Firebase Analytics** help you understand how users are interacting with your app. You can track events like:

- Button clicks

- Screen views

- Feature usage

Firebase Analytics is easy to integrate and can provide insights into which features are used most and where users are dropping off.

4. Pro Tip: Handling Negative Reviews Effectively

4.1 Why Negative Reviews Matter

Negative reviews can significantly affect your app's **reputation** and **download rates**. However, they also provide an opportunity to **improve** and **engage with users**. Addressing issues highlighted in negative reviews shows that you care about user feedback and can help improve your app's ratings.

4.2 Best Practices for Managing Negative Reviews

1. Respond Promptly and Professionally

Respond to negative reviews **within a reasonable timeframe** to show that you value user feedback. Stay polite and avoid being defensive. Acknowledge the issue, and, if necessary, provide a solution or timeline for a fix.

2. Use In-App Feedback

Encourage users to report issues through **in-app feedback** before they leave a public review. This provides a chance to resolve the issue privately and potentially prevent negative reviews.

3. Keep Track of Issues

If the same issues keep appearing in multiple reviews, track them in a **bug tracker** or **task management tool**. Work on resolving these problems quickly.

4. Offer Solutions

Always provide **actionable solutions** in your responses. For example, if users are experiencing crashes, acknowledge the bug and let them know when an update with a fix will be released.

FINAL PROJECT: BUILDING A COMPLETE AI-POWERED APP

Chapter 15: The Future of Android Development

Android development has come a long way since its inception, and it continues to evolve rapidly with each new release. As Android developers, it's essential to stay on top of the latest trends, tools, and innovations to remain competitive and leverage new opportunities for building **smarter, more efficient, and more engaging apps**.

In this chapter, we will explore the future of Android development, focusing on:

- **Android 15 & Beyond: What's Changing?**

- **Kotlin Multiplatform** (Write once, run on Android & iOS)

- **AI-powered App Development & Automation**

- **Expert Insights**: Predictions from top Android developers

By the end of this chapter, you will have a clear understanding of the **exciting trends** shaping the future of Android development and how you can **prepare your apps for the next generation** of Android technologies.

1. Android 15 & Beyond: What's Changing?

1.1 The Evolution of Android

Since Android's launch in 2008, it has undergone numerous changes, with each new version introducing **innovative features** and **performance improvements**. From the introduction of **material design** to **support for foldable devices**, the Android ecosystem has continuously expanded to meet new market demands and technological advancements.

As we look toward **Android 15 and beyond**, there are several key changes expected to impact the Android ecosystem.

1.2 Key Features in Android 15 and Future Releases

Android 15 is likely to introduce **several significant updates** that will continue to shape the way developers approach app development. Here are some anticipated features:

1.2.1 Enhanced AI and Machine Learning Integration

AI and **machine learning** (ML) are expected to be even more integrated into Android apps. **Android 15** will likely have enhanced support for **on-device AI** (using frameworks like **TensorFlow Lite** and **ML Kit**), making it easier to build apps that leverage intelligent capabilities like **image recognition**, **natural language processing**, and **recommendation systems**.

1.2.2 Foldable and Multi-Window Support

With foldable devices on the rise, **Android 15** is expected to offer even better **multi-window and foldable device** support, allowing developers to create apps that seamlessly adapt to **different screen configurations**. This will include enhanced APIs for **multi-resume** and **split-screen experiences**, enabling a more flexible, responsive, and immersive user experience.

1.2.3 Improved App Performance and Battery Efficiency

Google has always focused on improving **app performance** and **battery efficiency** in Android releases, and **Android 15** will continue this trend. Expect more powerful tools to optimize the **runtime performance** of your apps, including better **memory management**, **background process optimizations**, and **battery consumption reduction**.

1.2.4 Native Support for Wearables and IoT

With the rise of **smartwatches** and **IoT devices**, Android is moving towards deeper **integration with wearables** and **connected devices**. Android 15 may include new **APIs** and **SDKs** to help developers create cross-platform apps that work seamlessly across Android smartphones, wearables, and IoT devices.

1.2.5 Privacy and Security Enhancements

Android 15 will likely continue to refine **privacy and security** features. Expect enhanced **data protection tools**, **privacy features**, and **transparent app permission handling**, allowing users to control how their data is accessed and shared. This will include tighter regulations on **background location tracking** and **sensor data** access, further promoting **user privacy**.

1.3 The Transition to Android 15: What Developers Need to Know

- **Backward Compatibility**: Google will ensure that apps built for **previous Android versions** (Android 12,

13, and 14) continue to function smoothly on Android 15. However, you will need to **test and update** your apps to take full advantage of the new features and optimizations.

- **API Updates**: Android 15 will introduce **new and deprecated APIs**. You will need to familiarize yourself with the updated APIs to ensure that your apps remain **efficient** and **compatible**.

- **Developer Tools**: Expect new developer tools and **Android Studio updates** that will enable faster and more efficient app development, including **debugging tools, UI design support**, and **device emulators**.

2. Kotlin Multiplatform: Write Once, Run on Android & iOS

2.1 What is Kotlin Multiplatform?

Kotlin Multiplatform (KMP) is a groundbreaking technology that allows developers to share **code across platforms**, such as **Android, iOS, web**, and even **desktop** applications. KMP allows you to write a single **shared codebase** while still utilizing platform-specific features and functionality.

Instead of writing separate code for Android and iOS, Kotlin Multiplatform allows you to **re-use business logic**, **data models**, and other non-UI components across platforms, saving development time and effort. This approach simplifies the process of building and maintaining cross-platform apps.

2.2 How Kotlin Multiplatform Works

Kotlin Multiplatform uses **shared code** for logic and **platform-specific code** for user interfaces (UI). This allows developers to write platform-independent code while still being able to access platform-specific APIs when necessary.

How Kotlin Multiplatform Works in Practice:

1. **Shared Code**:

   Business logic, data models, networking code, and algorithms can all be written in Kotlin and shared between Android and iOS.

2. **Platform-Specific Code**:

UI code, file system access, and other platform-specific features can still be written using platform-specific languages and frameworks (e.g., Swift for iOS, Kotlin for Android).

Example: Sharing a Networking Module

kotlin

```
// Shared code (Kotlin)

expect fun getNetworkClient(): HttpClient


// Android implementation (Kotlin)

actual fun getNetworkClient(): HttpClient {

    return HttpClient(Android)

}


// iOS implementation (Swift)

actual fun getNetworkClient(): HttpClient {
```

```
    return HttpClient(Ios)

}
```

2.3 Benefits of Kotlin Multiplatform ·

1. **Write Once, Run Anywhere**:

   With Kotlin Multiplatform, you can **share up to 80%** of your app's codebase between Android and iOS.

2. **Native Performance**:

   Since you still write platform-specific code for the UI, the app performs as **efficiently** as native apps built with Android or iOS development tools.

3. **Seamless Interoperability**:

   Kotlin Multiplatform allows easy **interoperability** with both Android and iOS libraries. You can still use existing **platform-specific libraries** when needed, while sharing the majority of your app's codebase.

4. **Faster Time to Market**:

Since you're sharing a large portion of the codebase, you can significantly **reduce development time**, resulting in faster **time to market** for both platforms.

2.4 When to Use Kotlin Multiplatform

Kotlin Multiplatform is ideal for:

- **Apps with similar functionality on both Android and iOS**: If your app shares significant logic and features across both platforms, KMP is an excellent choice.

- **Cross-platform business logic**: For apps where most functionality is independent of the UI (such as banking apps, social media apps, and ecommerce platforms), KMP can provide a highly efficient solution.

However, if your app heavily relies on **complex platform-specific UI** or involves frequent use of **platform-specific APIs** (such as those for sensors, camera, or notifications), you may want to reconsider KMP or limit its scope.

3. AI-Powered App Development & Automation

3.1 The Role of AI in Modern Android Development

AI and **machine learning (ML)** are increasingly being used to improve app performance, enhance user experiences, and automate tedious tasks. AI-powered features such as **personalized recommendations**, **voice assistants**, **image recognition**, and **chatbots** are transforming how apps interact with users.

As **AI capabilities improve**, Android developers will be able to build **smarter apps** that:

- **Understand user behavior** and adapt to their needs

- **Personalize content** and offer tailored experiences

- **Analyze user-generated content** for feedback and insights

- **Automate app functions** for efficiency and performance

3.2 Implementing AI in Android Apps

Using TensorFlow Lite for On-Device Machine Learning

TensorFlow Lite allows you to run machine learning models on Android devices, enabling **on-device predictions** for things like **image classification, language processing**, and **speech recognition**. It provides a framework for creating **AI-powered features** while maintaining **speed, privacy**, and **offline functionality**.

ML Kit for Pre-Built Models

Firebase ML Kit provides a collection of **pre-built models** for common AI tasks, including:

- **Text recognition (OCR)**: Extract text from images.

- **Face detection**: Detect faces in images and videos.

- **Barcode scanning**: Scan and recognize barcodes.

- **Language identification**: Identify languages from text input.

AI-Powered Automation

AI and **machine learning** can automate various aspects of app development, including:

- **Automating testing**: Using AI to generate **test cases** and **automated UI tests**.

- **App optimization**: AI-driven tools can suggest performance improvements, such as reducing resource usage or optimizing code paths.

- **User engagement**: AI can analyze user interactions to predict their next actions and trigger events based on their behavior.

3.3 Future of AI in Android Development

As AI technologies evolve, Android apps will continue to become **more intelligent**, offering:

- **Smarter user interfaces** that can **predict needs** and make recommendations.

- **Automated workflows** for users, reducing friction and improving efficiency.

- **Better user interaction**, such as **natural language processing** for voice-based commands and **gesture control** for hands-free interaction.

4. Expert Insights: Predictions from Top Android Developers

4.1 Expert Insights on the Future of Android Development

1. Kotlin Will Continue to Lead

Many top developers predict that **Kotlin** will remain the **primary language** for Android development. As Google continues to invest in Kotlin, developers will have access to **new language features** that simplify app development and improve productivity.

2. Jetpack Compose Will Revolutionize UI Development

Jetpack Compose, the modern **UI toolkit** for Android, will likely **replace XML-based layouts** in favor of a more **declarative approach** to building UIs. This will make Android UIs more **reactive** and **dynamic**, similar to how React works for web development.

3. Cross-Platform Development Will Grow

With **Kotlin Multiplatform**, **Flutter**, and **React Native**, the trend toward **cross-platform development** is set to grow. However, developers will still face challenges in terms of performance and **UI consistency**, which will shape the evolution of these frameworks.

4. AI & Automation Will Transform App Development

As **AI** and **machine learning** continue to evolve, more Android apps will incorporate **intelligent features**. From **automated testing** to **AI-powered personalization**, developers will have the tools to create more **adaptive and efficient apps**.

Chapter 16: AI-Powered Social Media App – Part 1 (Backend & Authentication)

Building an **AI-powered social media app** is an ambitious yet incredibly rewarding challenge. In this chapter, we will focus on the **backend** aspects of the app, including **user authentication**, **database design**, **real-time chat** and **notifications**, and how to implement **AI-powered personalized content recommendations**. These elements will lay the foundation for a seamless and engaging user experience, allowing your app to scale efficiently while providing users with personalized content.

This chapter will be divided into the following key sections:

- **User authentication with Firebase Auth**

- **Database design for scalable AI-driven social apps**

- **Implementing real-time chat & notifications**

- **AI-powered personalized content recommendations**

By the end of this chapter, you will have built a robust backend system capable of handling user authentication, content management, real-time communication, and AI-based recommendations—all critical elements for the success of a social media platform.

1. User Authentication with Firebase Auth

1.1 What is Firebase Authentication?

Firebase Authentication provides an easy and secure way to manage users in your app. It supports multiple authentication methods such as **email/password, Google Sign-In, Facebook Login**, and more. Firebase Auth handles **signing up users, signing in users**, and managing **password resets**, all while maintaining **security** and **scalability**.

For a social media app, **user authentication** is essential as it ensures that users can securely log in, manage their profiles, and access personalized content. Firebase Authentication simplifies this process by offering a **unified solution** that works across **Android, iOS, and the web**.

1.2 Setting Up Firebase Authentication

To begin using **Firebase Authentication** in your Android app, follow these steps:

Step 1: Add Firebase to Your Android Project

1. Go to the Firebase Console, create a new project, and add your app.

2. Download the **google-services.json** file and place it in the **app folder** of your project.

3. Add the necessary dependencies in your **build.gradle** file:

gradle

```
dependencies {
    implementation 'com.google.firebase:firebase-auth:21.0.1'
}
```

Step 2: Initialize Firebase Authentication In your **MainActivity** or **App Initialization** code, initialize Firebase:

kotlin

```
FirebaseApp.initializeApp(this)
```

Step 3: Implement User Registration and Login Firebase Auth supports various sign-in methods. Below is an example of **email and password authentication**:

- **Sign-Up (Email and Password):**

kotlin

```kotlin
val email = "user@example.com"

val password = "password123"

FirebaseAuth.getInstance().createUserWithEmailAndPassword(email, password)
    .addOnCompleteListener(this) { task ->
        if (task.isSuccessful) {
            // User registration successful
        } else {
            // Handle failure
        }
    }
```

- **Sign-In (Email and Password):**

kotlin

```kotlin
FirebaseAuth.getInstance().signInWithEmailAndPassword(email, password)
    .addOnCompleteListener(this) { task ->
        if (task.isSuccessful) {
            // User login successful
        } else {
            // Handle failure
        }
    }
```

Step 4: Implement Password Reset

kotlin

```kotlin
val email = "user@example.com"

FirebaseAuth.getInstance().sendPasswordResetEmail(email)
```

```
.addOnCompleteListener { task ->

    if (task.isSuccessful) {

        // Password reset email sent

    } else {

        // Handle failure

    }

}
```

Firebase Authentication also supports other methods like **Google Sign-In**, **Facebook Login**, and **Phone Authentication**. You can choose whichever method best fits your app's user experience.

1.3 Best Practices for Firebase Authentication

- **Secure Password Storage**: Firebase stores passwords in a **hashed and salted format**, which prevents exposing users' sensitive information.

- **Two-Factor Authentication**: Implement **2FA** for users to add an extra layer of security.

- **Error Handling**: Provide **clear error messages** for authentication failures, such as invalid credentials or account not found.

2. Database Design for Scalable AI-Driven Social Apps

2.1 The Role of the Database in Social Media Apps

The **database** serves as the backbone of a social media app. It stores data related to users, posts, comments, messages, and more. For an **AI-driven social media app**, the database must be designed to handle **large-scale data**, as well as support features like **real-time communication** and **personalized content**.

Firebase offers two popular **cloud databases**: **Firebase Realtime Database** and **Cloud Firestore**. Cloud Firestore is generally preferred due to its **flexibility**, **scalability**, and **advanced querying capabilities**.

2.2 Structuring the Database

For an AI-driven social app, you need to structure your database to support various functionalities such as **user profiles, posts, comments, likes,** and **content recommendations**.

Here's a sample **Firestore database structure**:

markdown

/users/{userId}

   - username

   - email

   - profileImage

   - bio

   - followers (array of userIds)

   - following (array of userIds)

   - recommendedContent (array of postIds)

/posts/{postId}

- userId

- content (text or media)

- timestamp

- likes (array of userIds)

- comments (array of commentIds)

/comments/{commentId}

- userId

- postId

- commentText

- timestamp

/notifications/{notificationId}

- userId

- message

- type (like, comment, follow)

- readStatus

- timestamp

Explanation:

- The **/users** collection stores user profile information, including **followers**, **following**, and recommended content.

- The **/posts** collection contains posts made by users, along with the **likes** and **comments**.

- The **/comments** collection stores user comments on posts.

- The **/notifications** collection is used for managing notifications like new likes or comments.

2.3 Ensuring Scalability

For an AI-driven app with thousands of users, scalability is crucial. Here are some strategies to ensure your app can handle growth:

- **Sharding**: Break large datasets into smaller **subcollections** to distribute the load efficiently.

- **Indexing**: Use Firestore's built-in indexing system to speed up queries, especially for **timestamp-based filtering** or **recommending content**.

- **Paginated Queries**: To avoid loading too much data at once, implement **pagination** for queries that return large datasets, like the posts feed or user comments.

3. Implementing Real-Time Chat & Notifications

3.1 Real-Time Chat System

A real-time chat system is essential for any social media app. Firebase offers **Firebase Realtime Database** and **Firestore** for implementing real-time chat. For chat functionality, we'll use **Firestore** because of its **real-time syncing capabilities**.

Step 1: Creating a Chat Collection

You can structure the chat database as follows:

markdown

```
/chats/{chatId}
```

- userIds (array of userIds)

- lastMessage

- timestamp

- messages (subcollection)

/messages/{messageId}

- senderId

- messageContent

- timestamp

Step 2: Sending and Receiving Messages

To send a message, add a document to the /messages subcollection:

kotlin

```kotlin
val chatRef = db.collection("chats").document(chatId)
val message = hashMapOf(
    "senderId" to senderId,
```

```kotlin
    "messageContent" to messageText,

    "timestamp" to FieldValue.serverTimestamp()

)

chatRef.collection("messages").add(message)
```

To listen for new messages in real-time:

kotlin

```kotlin
chatRef.collection("messages")

    .orderBy("timestamp")

    .addSnapshotListener { snapshot, exception ->

        if (exception != null || snapshot == null)
return@addSnapshotListener

        for (document in snapshot) {

            val message = document.data["messageContent"] as
String

            // Update chat UI with new message

        }
```

}

This will allow real-time message updates for users, with the latest messages appearing instantly in the app.

3.2 Push Notifications

Push notifications keep users engaged by notifying them of important events like **new messages**, **likes**, or **comments**.

You can integrate **Firebase Cloud Messaging (FCM)** to send notifications.

Step 1: Set Up Firebase Cloud Messaging

Add the necessary FCM dependency to your build.gradle:

gradle

```
dependencies {
    implementation            'com.google.firebase:firebase-messaging:23.0.0'
}
```

Step 2: Send Push Notifications

To send a notification when a new message is received:

kotlin

```kotlin
val message =
RemoteMessage.Builder("user_token@fcm.googleapis.com")
    .setMessageId(messageId)
    .addData("title", "New Message")
    .addData("body", "You have a new message")
    .build()


FirebaseMessaging.getInstance().send(message)
```

Step 3: Handling Notifications in the App

To display push notifications to the user, implement a FirebaseMessagingService:

kotlin

```kotlin
class            MyFirebaseMessagingService            :
FirebaseMessagingService() {

    override    fun    onMessageReceived(remoteMessage:
RemoteMessage) {

        // Handle the received message and display notification

    }

}
```

This allows your app to send real-time push notifications, keeping users engaged.

4. AI-Powered Personalized Content Recommendations

4.1 What Are Personalized Content Recommendations?

AI-powered content recommendations provide users with personalized feeds based on their interests, past behavior, and preferences. For a social media app, this can include recommending posts, users to follow, or groups to join based on **likes**, **shares**, and **comments**.

4.2 Building the Recommendation System

To implement personalized content recommendations, you can use machine learning models such as **collaborative filtering**, **content-based filtering**, or a **hybrid approach**. For simplicity, let's focus on a basic content-based recommendation system.

Step 1: Collect User Interactions Data

Track interactions like:

- Which posts the user has liked
- Which content they've commented on
- Content that they've viewed for longer periods

Step 2: Build a Simple Recommendation Algorithm

A simple algorithm might use **Cosine Similarity** or **Collaborative Filtering** to recommend posts based on what similar users have liked.

For example, if a user frequently likes **sports-related posts**, the system can recommend similar posts from other users who share similar interests.

kotlin

```
val recommendedPosts = posts.filter { post ->

   userLikes.contains(post.category)

}
```

Step 3: Deploy AI Models

For more sophisticated recommendations, you can deploy machine learning models like **Matrix Factorization** or **Neural Networks** using **TensorFlow Lite** or **Firebase ML Kit**. These models can be used to predict which content a user is likely to interact with next based on their historical data.

Chapter 17: AI-Powered Social Media App – Part 2 (Frontend & UX Optimization)

Creating an AI-powered social media app requires a seamless and engaging **frontend**, with a **clean, responsive UI** and **smooth user experience (UX)**. After building the backend features in Part 1, such as **user authentication**, **real-time chat**, and **content recommendations**, it's time to shift focus to the **UI design** and **user interactions**. This part will help you design an **intuitive frontend** that ensures users enjoy using your app and are engaged for the long term.

In this chapter, we will cover:

- **Designing an engaging UI with Jetpack Compose**

- **Adding like, comment, and follow features**

- **Push notifications with Firebase Cloud Messaging (FCM)**

- Using AI for auto-tagging and user engagement predictions

- Final Challenge: Deploy your app and share it online

By the end of this chapter, you'll have the tools and knowledge to build an **interactive frontend**, create **personalized experiences**, and optimize your app's **user interface** for maximum engagement.

1. Designing an Engaging UI with Jetpack Compose

1.1 Why Use Jetpack Compose for UI Development?

Jetpack Compose is Android's modern, **declarative UI toolkit** that simplifies UI development by allowing developers to design UIs using **Kotlin** programming language. Unlike XML-based layouts, Jetpack Compose enables **dynamic UI** building and **real-time updates** by simply describing how the UI should look based on the app's state. It is flexible, highly extensible, and allows for cleaner and more maintainable code.

Key Benefits of Jetpack Compose:

- **Less Boilerplate**: No need to define XML layouts; everything is done in Kotlin code.

- **Declarative UI**: You define UI components based on app state, and Compose automatically handles updates.

- **Improved Productivity**: The live previews, interactive UI debugging, and built-in tools make UI design more efficient.

1.2 Getting Started with Jetpack Compose

To start using Jetpack Compose in your project, you need to add the appropriate dependencies in your build.gradle file.

gradle

```
dependencies {
    implementation 'androidx.compose.ui:ui:1.1.0'
    implementation 'androidx.compose.material:material:1.1.0'
    implementation 'androidx.compose.ui:ui-tooling-preview:1.1.0'
}
```

Then, in your **MainActivity** or the **App's entry point**, set up the basic Compose structure:

kotlin

```
setContent {
    MyApp()
}
```

```kotlin
@Composable

fun MyApp() {

    // UI Components go here

    Text(text = "Welcome to the AI-powered Social App")

}
```

1.3 Designing the App Layout with Jetpack Compose

1.3.1 Creating the Main Screen Layout

For a social media app, the **main screen** typically consists of:

- A **top navigation bar**

- A **feed of posts**

- **User profile icon**

- **Floating action button (FAB)** for creating new posts

Here's an example layout using Jetpack Compose:

kotlin

```kotlin
@Composable
```

```kotlin
fun MainScreen() {

    Scaffold(

        topBar = {

            TopAppBar(

                title = { Text(text = "AI Social Media") },

                actions = {

                    IconButton(onClick = { /* Handle profile click */
}) {

                        Icon(Icons.Default.AccountCircle,
contentDescription = "Profile")

                    }

                }

            )

        },

        floatingActionButton = {

            FloatingActionButton(onClick = { /* Create post */ })
{
```

```kotlin
                Icon(Icons.Default.Add,    contentDescription    =
"Create Post")

            }

        },

        content = {

            PostFeed()  // Feed of posts to be displayed here

        }

    )

}
```

1.3.2 Building the Post Feed UI

The **PostFeed** UI displays the posts of users, including text, images, and actions like **likes**, **comments**, and **shares**. We can create this UI with **LazyColumn**, a composable that efficiently displays a vertical list.

kotlin

```kotlin
@Composable

fun PostFeed(posts: List<Post>) {
```

```kotlin
LazyColumn {

    items(posts) { post ->

        PostItem(post)

    }

  }

}


@Composable

fun PostItem(post: Post) {

  Column(modifier = Modifier.padding(16.dp)) {

    Text(text    =    post.userName,    fontWeight    =
FontWeight.Bold)

    Text(text = post.content)

    Image(painter = rememberImagePainter(post.imageUrl),
contentDescription = "Post Image")

    Row {

      IconButton(onClick = { /* Like post */ }) {
```

```
        Icon(Icons.Default.Favorite,  contentDescription  =
"Like")

      }

      IconButton(onClick = { /* Comment on post */ }) {

        Icon(Icons.Default.Comment, contentDescription =
"Comment")

      }

    }

  }

}
```

In this example, **PostFeed** iterates over a list of posts and displays each post's details, including the **user name**, **post content**, **image**, and interaction buttons for **liking** and **commenting**.

1.4 Animations and Transitions with Jetpack Compose

Jetpack Compose also supports **animations** that can enhance the user experience, such as animating the **like button** when clicked or transitioning between screens smoothly. You can use AnimatedVisibility, animateDpAsState, and other Compose animation tools to create dynamic UI transitions.

kotlin

```
@Composable
fun LikeButton(liked: Boolean) {
    val transition = updateTransition(liked, label = "")
    val scale by transition.animateFloat(
        label = "scale",
        transitionSpec = { tween(durationMillis = 300) }
    ) { if (liked) 1.2f else 1f }

    IconButton(onClick = { /* Like the post */ }) {
        Icon(
            imageVector = Icons.Default.Favorite,
            contentDescription = "Like",
            modifier = Modifier.scale(scale)
```

```
        )

    }

}
```

This snippet animates the **like button** when the user taps it, making it scale up briefly before returning to its normal size.

2. Adding Like, Comment, and Follow Features

2.1 Like Feature

The **Like** feature allows users to express approval for a post. It typically involves:

- Toggling the **like button** when clicked

- Updating the **like count** in the database

Here's a simple implementation:

kotlin

```
var liked by remember { mutableStateOf(false) }
```

LikeButton(liked) { liked = !liked }

To sync this with your database (Firestore), you would update the likes array when a user clicks the like button:

kotlin

```
fun toggleLike(postId: String) {

    val                          postRef                          =
FirebaseFirestore.getInstance().collection("posts").document(
postId)

    postRef.update("likes",
FieldValue.arrayUnion(currentUserId))

}
```

2.2 Comment Feature

The **Comment** feature allows users to share their thoughts on a post. It requires:

- A **text input field** to write comments

- Displaying comments below the post

kotlin

```kotlin
var commentText by remember { mutableStateOf("") }
```

```kotlin
TextField(
    value = commentText,
    onValueChange = { commentText = it },
    label = { Text("Write a comment...") },
    modifier = Modifier.fillMaxWidth()
)
```

To store comments in the database:

kotlin

```kotlin
fun postComment(postId: String, commentText: String) {
    val comment = hashMapOf(
        "userId" to currentUserId,
        "commentText" to commentText,
```

```kotlin
        "timestamp" to FieldValue.serverTimestamp()
    )

    val                    postRef                    =
FirebaseFirestore.getInstance().collection("posts").document(
postId)

    postRef.collection("comments").add(comment)
}
```

2.3 Follow Feature

The **Follow** feature allows users to follow other users and see their posts in their feed. This involves:

- Updating the **followers** and **following** arrays in the user's profile

- Displaying **follow/unfollow** buttons based on the user's relationship

kotlin

```kotlin
fun toggleFollow(userId: String) {
```

```kotlin
val                          userRef                          =
FirebaseFirestore.getInstance().collection("users").document(
currentUserId)

    userRef.update(

        "following", FieldValue.arrayUnion(userId)

    )

}
```

3. Push Notifications with Firebase Cloud Messaging (FCM)

3.1 Setting Up Firebase Cloud Messaging

Firebase Cloud Messaging (FCM) is a service that allows you to send notifications to users in real time. Whether it's for new **messages**, **likes**, or **comments**, FCM ensures that users remain engaged with your app.

Step 1: Adding FCM to Your Project

Add FCM dependencies to your **build.gradle** file:

gradle

```
dependencies {

    implementation                'com.google.firebase:firebase-
messaging:23.0.0'

}
```

Step 2: Sending Notifications

To send notifications, you'll need to use the **FCM API**. For example, when a user likes a post, you can send a notification to the post owner:

kotlin

```
val                    message                    =
RemoteMessage.Builder("recipient_token@fcm.googleapis.c
om")

    .setMessageId(messageId)

    .addData("title", "New Like")

    .addData("body", "Someone liked your post!")

    .build()
```

```kotlin
FirebaseMessaging.getInstance().send(message)
```

3.2 Handling Notifications in the App

Create a **FirebaseMessagingService** to handle incoming notifications:

kotlin

```kotlin
class MyFirebaseMessagingService : FirebaseMessagingService() {

    override fun onMessageReceived(remoteMessage: RemoteMessage) {

        val title = remoteMessage.data["title"]

        val body = remoteMessage.data["body"]

        showNotification(title, body)

    }


    private fun showNotification(title: String?, body: String?) {
```

```kotlin
val                notificationManager            =
getSystemService(Context.NOTIFICATION_SERVICE)    as
NotificationManager

val  notification  =  NotificationCompat.Builder(this,
"default")

    .setContentTitle(title)

    .setContentText(body)

    .setSmallIcon(R.drawable.ic_notification)

    .build()


notificationManager.notify(0, notification)

  }

}
```

4. Using AI for Auto-Tagging and User Engagement Predictions

4.1 Auto-Tagging Content

Auto-tagging helps categorize posts based on their content. AI models can analyze text and images in posts to assign relevant tags. For example, if a user uploads a photo of a beach, the AI might automatically tag it with "beach," "vacation," and "sunset."

You can use **TensorFlow Lite** for image recognition and **Natural Language Processing (NLP)** for text tagging. For instance:

kotlin

```kotlin
fun generateTags(post: Post) {

    val tags = mutableListOf<String>()


    if (post.imageUrl != null) {
        // Run image recognition to identify objects in the image
        tags.add("beach")
    }
```

```kotlin
if (post.content.contains("vacation")) {

    tags.add("vacation")

}


    updatePostWithTags(post.id, tags)

}
```

4.2 Predicting User Engagement

AI can predict which content will likely engage users based on their behavior. For instance, a recommendation algorithm can suggest posts to a user based on **likes**, **shares**, and **comments**.

Using **machine learning models**, you can train a model that predicts the likelihood of a user engaging with a particular post:

kotlin

```kotlin
fun predictEngagement(user: User, post: Post): Double {

    // Feed user behavior and post features into an AI model

    return model.predict(user, post)
```

}

This can help improve the **personalization** of content feeds.

5. Final Challenge: Deploy Your App & Share It Online

5.1 Deploying Your App

Once your app is ready, it's time to deploy it! Follow these steps:

1. **Build a signed APK or AAB** using Android Studio.

2. **Set up your app's Play Store listing**, including the **title**, **description**, and **screenshots**.

3. **Upload your app** to the **Google Play Console** and submit it for review.

5.2 Share It Online

After your app is live, share it on social media, developer forums, and app review sites to gain traction. Encourage users to provide feedback through **reviews** and **ratings**.

Appendix: Bonus Resources

Writing Tips for Developers

As a developer, writing clean, maintainable, and understandable code is as important as the code itself. It's not just about making the app work; it's about **creating code that is easy to understand**, **modify**, and **expand**. In addition to writing efficient code, developers must also produce **documentation** that communicates how the code works and why specific design decisions were made. This helps the development team, future developers, and even yourself, in case you need to revisit the code after some time.

This appendix will provide practical **writing tips** on:

- **How to write clean, readable documentation**

- **Best practices for code comments and structuring projects**

- **The importance of writing for maintainability**

By following these guidelines, you will ensure your code is **robust**, **scalable**, and **easy to work with**, whether you're collaborating with a team or maintaining your own projects.

1. How to Write Clean, Readable Documentation

1.1 Why Documentation Matters

Documentation is essential for several reasons:

- **Communication**: It allows developers (including your future self) to understand your code.

- **Collaboration**: It helps team members understand the codebase without needing to ask constant questions.

- **Knowledge Transfer**: If someone new joins the project, clear documentation accelerates the learning process.

- **Ease of Maintenance**: Well-documented code is easier to debug, update, and extend.

1.2 Types of Documentation

There are two main types of documentation you should focus on:

1. **Inline Documentation**: This is documentation that explains specific parts of your code. It's written directly

within the code itself (e.g., function descriptions, variables, and logic explanation).

2. **External Documentation**: This is documentation that explains the overall structure of the app, how the app works, API documentation, and design decisions. It is typically stored in markdown files or hosted online (e.g., README files, API docs).

1.3 Best Practices for Writing Documentation

- **Be Clear and Concise**: Documentation should provide enough context for someone to understand the code, without being overly verbose. Be specific about the **what**, **why**, and **how** of the code, but avoid unnecessary details.

Example:

kotlin

```
// Good Example: Explains what and why

// Calculates the total cost of an order, including taxes and discounts.
```

```
fun calculateTotal(order: Order): Double {

    val tax = order.amount * TAX_RATE

    val discount = if (order.hasDiscount) order.amount *
DISCOUNT_RATE else 0.0

    return order.amount + tax - discount

}
```

- **Use Consistent Terminology**: Use the same terminology throughout the documentation and comments. Avoid switching between terms for the same concept (e.g., using "cost" in some places and "price" in others).

- **Explain the "Why"**: While it's essential to describe what the code is doing, don't forget to explain why specific decisions were made. For example, if you chose a particular algorithm over another, explain the reasoning behind it.

- **Update Documentation Regularly**: Documentation should be updated whenever the code changes. If a function or module is updated, its documentation should reflect those changes immediately. **Outdated**

documentation is worse than no documentation because it can mislead developers and lead to errors.

- **Use Visual Aids**: Where applicable, **diagrams**, **flowcharts**, or **UML models** can provide visual explanations that help make the code easier to understand.

1.4 Example of Good Documentation

kotlin

```
/**

* Calculates the total price of an order after applying taxes and discounts.

*

* This function calculates the total price for an order by first applying

* a tax rate, then subtracting any eligible discount. The discount is

* only applied if the order has the "hasDiscount" flag set to true.
```

```
 *

 * @param order The order object containing the price and
discount eligibility.

 * @return The total price for the order after applying tax and
discount.

 */

fun calculateTotal(order: Order): Double {

    val tax = order.amount * TAX_RATE

    val discount = if (order.hasDiscount) order.amount *
DISCOUNT_RATE else 0.0

    return order.amount + tax - discount

}
```

2. Best Practices for Code Comments & Structuring Projects

2.1 Code Comments: When and How to Use Them

Code comments are a valuable tool for providing context and clarifying the intent of your code. However, over-commenting can make the code cluttered, while under-commenting can leave important logic unexplained. The key is balance.

When to Comment:

- **Complex logic**: If your code implements a complex algorithm or logic that isn't immediately obvious, explain the **how** and **why** behind it.

- **Edge cases**: If a function or method handles an edge case or does something unusual, document it so others don't make incorrect assumptions.

- **Workarounds**: If you implement a workaround or temporary solution, explain the reason and indicate when it should be revisited.

How to Comment:

- Use **block comments** for explanations that require more detail, such as documenting the purpose of a function or explaining complex logic.

- Use **inline comments** for smaller clarifications, such as explaining a variable's purpose or describing a specific condition.

Good Practice Example:

kotlin

```
// Inline comment for a simple operation

val discount = if (order.hasDiscount) order.amount * DISCOUNT_RATE else 0.0


/*

 * Block comment explaining complex logic

 * This algorithm uses a greedy approach to optimize the schedule.

 * We start by sorting tasks by their duration and assigning them to the earliest available slot.

 * This ensures that tasks with shorter durations get completed first, maximizing efficiency.

 */

fun optimizeSchedule(tasks: List<Task>): Schedule {

    // sorting logic here
```

}

2.2 Structuring Your Codebase

Well-structured codebases are easier to navigate, maintain, and scale. Here are some best practices:

1. **Organize Code by Feature**: Group files and modules by their functionality (e.g., authentication, userProfile, posts, comments). This way, developers can quickly find and modify code based on its function.

2. **Follow the Single Responsibility Principle (SRP)**: Each class or function should have one job or responsibility. This makes your code easier to understand and reduces the risk of bugs when changes are made.

3. **Modularize Your Code**: Break your app into **smaller modules** or **libraries** to isolate functionality. This makes it easier to maintain, test, and scale.

4. **Naming Conventions**: Consistent naming conventions are essential. Use descriptive names for variables, functions, classes, and files. Avoid single-letter variables or overly generic names like temp or foo.

Example File Structure:

bash

```
/app
 /src
  /main
   /java
    /com
     /socialmediaapp
      /auth        # Authentication logic
      /feed        # Post feed functionality
      /profile     # User profile functionality
      /comments    # Commenting system
      /notifications # Push notifications
```

3. The Importance of Writing for Maintainability

3.1 What is Maintainability?

Maintainability refers to the ease with which a developer can modify, extend, or debug an application. Writing maintainable code is essential for the long-term success of a project, especially as the codebase grows and evolves.

3.2 Writing for Maintainability

- **Avoid Hardcoding Values**: Use constants or variables instead of hardcoding values like URLs, API keys, or configuration values. This makes it easier to modify these values in the future without affecting the whole codebase.

Example:

kotlin

```
// Hardcoded value (Not maintainable)

val apiUrl = "https://api.example.com/v1/data"
```

```
// More maintainable solution using constants

const val API_URL = "https://api.example.com/v1/data"
```

- **Keep Functions Small and Focused**: Each function or method should **do one thing** and **do it well**. This makes your code easier to test, understand, and maintain.

- **Write Tests**: Test-driven development (TDD) or writing unit tests for your functions ensures that your code works as expected and makes it easier to detect issues during maintenance.

- **Use Version Control**: Always use **version control systems** (such as **Git**) to track changes to your codebase. This helps you keep track of changes, collaborate with others, and roll back changes if something goes wrong.

3.3 Refactoring for Maintainability

As your project evolves, you may need to refactor your code to **improve readability**, **remove duplication**, and **enhance performance**. **Refactoring** is an ongoing process, and writing maintainable code involves always being mindful of future modifications.

Additional Resources & Learning Path

- **Recommended books, blogs, and courses**

- **Top Android developer communities to join**

Final Thoughts & Next Steps

- **Encouragement to keep building & innovating**

- How to **turn your app into a real business**

- **Join the Android developer community & contribute!**